.

PARTNERSHIP IS THE NEW LEADERSHIP

**PARTNERSHIP
IS THE NEW
LEADERSHIP**

By

TY BENNETT

Foreword by
Dr. Nido Qubein
President of High Point University

Partnership Is The New Leadership

Published by United Graphics, Inc.

Ty Bennett
Leadership Inc.
3940 Traverse Mountain Blvd.
Lehi, UT 84043
Web: www.tybennett.com

ISBN 978-0-9962752-3-1 (hardcover)

Cover & Interior Design/Formatting by Vickie Swisher • Studio 20|20

"This book is dedicated to the leaders who have partnered with me throughout my life. Those who have mentored, taught, and inspired me to step up and live my purpose."

ACKNOWLEDGEMENTS

"My business today is speaking and writing. While I am the one on stage – there is an incredible group of people who help make all of this happen. I want to thank my team: Karen Harris, Shannyn Downey, Jessica Fortier, Rebecca Clark, Taryn Knorren, Helen Foulger, Chris Madsen and Jill Gulbranson for their belief in this message, their incredible work ethic and their constructive feedback.

I want to thank my editor and writing partner – Lee Benson. Lee's talent amazes me, but his integrity inspires me.

I want to thank the clients and friends who have opened their organizations up for me to study their leadership in action. There are too many to list here but you will see many of their stories and insights featured throughout the book.

And last but not least I want to thank my family, especially my wife Sarah, for their undying support, belief in me and encouragement for this work!"

ENDORSEMENTS

Each of the endorsements for this book come from active CEOs of organizations who have brought Ty Bennett in to share the message of *Partnership Is The New Leadership*. They have seen firsthand the influence this content has had on their leadership team and the positive impact it has made in their culture.

"Leadership today has evolved and is now a partnership revolution. Ty Bennett beautifully articulates how engaging with this generation of leaders drives loyalty and success."

— KEN PENDERY, *CEO of First Watch Restaurants*

"As a new generation of leaders emerge, new ideas also surface. The exponential changes in management also require new perspectives. Ty Bennett's book, *Partnership Is The New Leadership*, provides an in-depth and critical understanding of today's leadership model, against the background of increasingly complicated industries in the 2000s. This book is a must-read for those who will be charting the course for their organization."

— LARRY PEARSON, *CEO of Pearson Tire/Direct Tire*

"Ty Bennett effectively captures a new approach to leadership that creates the culture, influence and commitment that every leader desires. I highly recommend *Partnership Is The New Leadership* if you're looking to make a significant impact and to learn tangible techniques that will help you grow your leadership."

— CAROL DOVER, *President and CEO of the Florida Restaurant and Lodging Association*

"We have heard about 'holacracy' as a new form of organizational structure that brings flexibility and discipline to the workplace. It emerged as the millennials, who make up a majority of the workforce now, rejected the old command and control structure of the military/industrial complex that dominated the 1900s. *Partnership Is The New Leadership* is the glue that can make the holacracy model of the 2000s stick together and make organizations perform exceptionally."

— JIM CRYSTAL, *CEO of Revelry Agency*

"*Partnership Is The New Leadership* offers a fresh perspective and insight into the concept of leadership that will work for this generation. It offers insights to today's leaders that fresh, more engaging and definitely more effective style of leadership."

— NADER MASADEH, *CEO of Buffalo Wings & Rings*

"Ty Bennett speaks with clarity and energy; inspiring changed mindsets, renewed confidence, and the commitment to put the *Partnership Is The New Leadership* plan into action."

— TARA DAVEY, *Executive Director of CHART (Council For Hotel & Restaurant Trainers)*

"*Partnership Is The New Leadership* combines insight from today's most influential leaders to propose a fresh, more engaging and definitely more effective style of leadership."

— SCOT THOMPSON, *Chief Executive Officer & President of C&A Industries, Inc.*

"I have had the pleasure of watching Ty Bennett demonstrate true leadership as he has been a keynote speaker at Winsight Events. He clearly shows his leadership for me, and many others, in two words: "Follow Me."

Partnership Is The New Leadership teaches his leadership philosophy. Relationships have always been and always will be the most precious and important currency. And as Ty writes, partner based leadership is built on relationships.

I highly recommend this book!"

— DAVID JOBE, *President, Winsight Events*

"Ty's new book, *Partnership Is The New Leadership*, provides a masterful blending of leadership insight & skills for leaders to engage their teams on higher level. The message of partnership based on commitment, passion and loyalty helps guide a culture of success within organizations."

— BOB GLAIMO, *CEO of Silver Diner Restaurants*

"It is probably not a coincidence that Ty Bennett's latest & soon to be bestseller is titled "*Partnership Is The New Leadership.*" Focused on helping leaders gain real commitment from their workers, it is a textbook for managing in the 21st century, an era that requires collaboration, authentic communication, and genuine caring and belief in employees. Ty is one of the all time favorite speakers at our Best Practices events because he walks the talk of his books and workshops. Humble, genuine, caring, totally lacking in pretense despite his phenomenal success as an entrepreneur and a writer, Ty connects with his audiences on a level that is rare in business. Companies and individuals seeking to make 2016 their best year yet, should be certain to put *Partnership Is The New Leadership* on their holiday book lists."

— JONI THOMAS DOOLIN, *CEO & Founder, TDn2K*

"*Partnership Is The New Leadership* offers fresh perspective and insight into the concept of leadership that will work for this generation."

— DARYL SCHRAAD,
President, Kemin Animal Nutrition & Health North America

TABLE OF CONTENTS

FOREWORD

Ty Bennett writes an excellent book. Relevant. Easy to understand and apply in business and in life – as a corporate leader and as a community one too. Like me, you will undoubtedly learn valuable insights from the many surveys the author conducted with some really smart people.

Leaders create capacity, both quantitative and qualitative capacity. They inspire and grow people. They nurture and grow companies. They envision and strategize solid plans – and then execute on them with determination and commitment. Leaders make things happen.

Leaders understand and respect people. They build productive teamwork. They succeed in spite of adversity. They know how to separate fact from fiction. They are tenacious and focused. What would this world be without effective and impactful leaders?

This is an important book. It teaches us new concepts and it reminds us of our productive failures and our unproductive successes. It guides our thinking about how leaders create and interpret value and how they evolve intentional congruence in all they do.

High Point University is a perfect example of what Ty teaches. After a career of 30 years as an executive coach, a serial entrepreneur, author and professional speaker, I returned to my undergraduate alma mater to assume the leadership position of president. With faithful courage, a reasoned approach, and an entrepreneurial mindset we set out to attract an academic and administrative team that is destined to make extraordinary things happen.

We adopted new messaging: We believe in the art of the possible. We adopt the fundamentals and principles that built the United States in the first place. We are a God, family, and country school. We aim to plant seeds of greatness in the minds, hearts, and souls of our students. We prepare these students for the world as it is going to be. We weave students in to the family instead of weeding them out of the system. On and on. Messages that harbor positive thinking, collaborative fellowship, and a cooperative spirit. Amazing what happens when you believe there are no such things as unrealistic dreams – just unrealistic timelines!

Come see our campus. Meet our people. Experience extraordinary! Growth at every level beat all expectations, especially when it all happened with a sense of importance and urgency – even in the midst of the most disrupted times in the last seven decades … the Great Recession! America noticed. Parents and friends advocated the purpose and potential of this school and students flocked here to learn, to grow, to have a life filled with success and framed with significance.

Ty Bennett gets it. He has observed, studied, and analyzed what works – and what doesn't – in leadership. And in this book he shares it with clarity and conviction. Read. Learn. Enjoy.

— DR. NIDO QUBEIN, *President of High Point University*

PARTNERSHIP
IS THE NEW
LEADERSHIP

CHAPTER 1

PARTNERSHIP IS THE NEW LEADERSHIP

What Do You Want From Your People?

Over a five-year period I conducted a survey of more than 5,000 leaders. These men and women were in leadership positions at multiple industries and at every level, from supervisors to CEOs, from managers to C-suite executives.

In this survey I asked only one question:
- **As a leader – what do you want from your people?**
  - **More than 75 percent answered with the one word response of: Commitment.**

That's what we want, isn't it? We want our people to be dedicated, to be all-in. We want them to be passionate and loyal. We want them to give their very best because they want to, not because they have to. We want them to be committed.

But here is the key: people are not committed to jobs. The Bureau of Labor Statistics reports that today's average worker will hold ten different jobs before age 40 and will have fifteen to twenty jobs by the time they retire.

And people are not committed to companies.

People are ultimately committed to people. It's relationships that engender trust, respect, accountability and commitment.

The old adage said leadership is based on title, position or authority. But people don't follow titles – they follow people.

Have you ever heard the saying "People join companies but leave bosses?" It's the leadership they are committed to.

That's why in today's world, partnership is the new leadership.

A new economy requires a new approach to leadership, and if what we want as leaders, more than anything else, is the commitment of our people, then we need to partner with them in order to foster an environment that naturally creates that commitment.

Partnership is the new leadership.

20,000 Go On Strike

Recently two cousins began fighting over a family business. This isn't really newsworthy – if you have ever been involved in a family business then you know this is quite common. But what happened in this case was amazing.

Arthur T. Demoulas was the CEO of a successful 71-store supermarket chain based in Massachusetts called Market Basket. Arthur T. was not only CEO, he was part owner. He owned 49.5 percent of the business to be exact. The majority owner was his cousin Arthur S. Demoulas (it's already getting confusing – I know – but stay with me). Arthur S owned 50.5% of the grocery store chain. Arthur T. and Arthur S. had very different views on leadership and how to run their company. As majority owner, Arthur S. pressured the board and they forced Arthur T. out as CEO. Then something amazing happened. Over 20,000 employees and customers went on strike in support of Arthur T. Not only did they go on strike – they stopped food shipments from coming in and within weeks brought the business to a screeching halt. The stores looked like a scene out of a movie – empty shelves, no customers, no employees – just vacant.

Why would the employees of Market Basket risk everything to show commitment to their leader?

The answer is because Arthur T. understood things that Arthur S. didn't. Arthur S. believed that his employees were committed to Market Basket, but the truth is they were committed to their leader – Arthur T. You see, Arthur T. knew that partnership is the new leadership and he led that way. Arthur T. approved a $1,000-per-quarter tuition reimbursement for his people (an expense Arthur S. thought unnecessary). Arthur T. paid his entry level cashiers $12 an hour even though the state minimum wage was $8 an hour. Arthur T. had a personal relationship with his people, he knew them by name, had served each one of them in a variety of ways, and had built trust and respect. I found it amazing that every one of the employees who were interviewed while they were picketing recounted specific, personal experiences they had with Arthur T. They talked about him walking them to their car after a shift, or how he always asked them about their family, or greeted them by name when they came into work. They knew him and he knew them and they loved him for it.

Arthur S. believed the old adage that title (being the majority owner) gives you the right to be heard and followed.

But Arthur T. understood that the value you provide your people is what earns you the right to be heard and followed.

In today's world, culture ultimately drives business and the leader's job is to create and maintain that culture. Arthur T. worked extremely hard to create a culture within Market Basket. It's a culture that Arthur S. didn't understand because he never participated in it.

Arthur S. was an investor, but Arthur T. was their partner – he was their *leader*.

A few weeks after the strike began, Arthur T. successfully bought out his cousin and became the sole owner of Market Basket. He reinstated himself as CEO and the company righted itself and is back on track and thriving. At the time of this writing the chain was on track to do $4.6 billion in revenue for the year.

That is the kind of leadership that works in today's world.

What Stops Leaders From Making An Impact?

It isn't title, position or authority – that's not what leadership is based on.

And it can't be the fault of the team. Leadership drives the team.

I believe what stops most leaders are themselves. We get in our own way.

The 3 Biggest Stumbling Blocks for Leaders are these:
1. Self-interest
2. Ego
3. Apathy

1. Self-Interest

Leadership is not about you – it is about the people you lead. It is natural for all of us to think inwardly and worry about our own positioning, comfort and achievement, but that is not where influence is built. The leader who is willing to place other people's interests first, to think outward and to serve others is the leader who makes the biggest impact. I want you to think about your natural reactions. When something negative happens, what is your first response? Is it to think – how does this affect me? Or is your first instinct to think how this will affect those you lead? Leaders who want to make an impact have to be willing to give up their self-interest.

2. Ego

Ego makes a leader un-teachable and unapproachable – two leadership killers. Keeping your ego in check means making it about we not me. It means giving credit and taking responsibility.

If I were to ask what caused the financial crisis in 2008, what would you say? (Hint: The answer has nothing to do with money). A common belief is that it was incompetence that caused the fall, a lack of knowledge or skill needed to get the job done.

But if we believe it was incompetence that caused the financial collapse, then we are saying that everyone on Wall Street was an idiot, which may sound funny, but it's not true. The people working on Wall Street and those who contributed the most to the financial crisis were some of the most competent people out there. What caused the financial crisis wasn't incompetence but rather overconfidence.

Incompetence is the problem of the unprepared and the under-equipped.

Overconfidence is the problem of experts and leaders.

I heard Malcolm Gladwell speak recently and he talked about this concept and it really got me thinking.

When the experts and leaders on Wall Street became overconfident they began to make bad decisions, take unhealthy risk, think selfishly, and shut out all constructive feedback. It was overconfidence that caused the market to collapse and in many cases it is overconfidence that causes businesses to fail, nations to falter and major crises to occur.

So what is the remedy for this problem facing the experts and leaders of today?

Humility.

What does humility do?

- It keeps your ego at bay while remaining confident in your capabilities.
- It makes you more concerned about what is right than who is right.
- It embraces new truth rather than defending outdated position.
- It ensures we never stop learning, growing, or listening.

Overconfidence causes us to lose perspective. Humility, the art of being humble, is the anecdote to overconfidence. Something every competent expert and leader needs.

3. Apathy
Leadership that makes an impact requires hard work, focus, discipline, and sacrifice. Leaders can't be apathetic in their approach and only do what is required. It's the extra effort that earns the greatest reward.

Would You Win Leader of The Year?

If there was a contest today and your employees, team members or clients were asked to vote, would you win Leader of the Year?

If you were asked to vote, what would make the Leader of the Year in your mind? Would it be their knowledge, their skillset, their example, their commitment, or the way they treated their people?

My daughter Andie is in third grade. She has loved school every year and done well. She has loved every teacher she has had. This year, however, her teacher, Mrs. Allison Moschetti, is her absolute favorite.

Mrs. Moschetti was just voted Teacher of the Year, so it isn't just Andie who thinks she is doing a great job. And I think we can learn a couple of things about leadership from her that has set her apart from her peers.

Before the school year started, we got a phone call from Mrs. Moschetti, who introduced herself, told us how excited she was to be Andie's teacher, and then scheduled an appointment to come and meet with us and Andie in our home. She came over and spent about 30 minutes with us. She got to know Andie mostly, although we all had great conversation. She asked what our expectations were for the year, what Andie's expectations were, what concerns we had, what concerns she had, and what she was looking forward to.

I was completely blown away by this home visit! I started to think about it. She has 30 kids in her classroom. If she was going to meet with each of them in their homes before school started, she was dedicating more than 15 hours of her summer vacation. I have heard so many teachers take the position that, "If I got paid more, I would try harder." *That is not leadership. That is victim mentality.* Leaders do more. And because of who they are and what they do – because of how much they care – they stand out.

I asked Mrs. Moschetti why she did the in-home visit and she said, "My goal is to partner with your daughter to create an incredible school year. I need to get to know her and to get to know you. I want to see her circumstances at home because it helps me to understand where she is coming from. And most importantly I want her to know that I love her and am excited to be her teacher."

I was sold after the in-home visit. Here's why: if a leader is willing to go above and beyond, they will typically make an impact. I also believe, the same as Mrs. Moschetti, that partnership is the new leadership. She approached teaching as a partnership with her students the same way every great leader needs to approach leadership as a partnership with their people. And I also love the fact that what drove her leadership was love. Before she really knew Andie, she loved her. Why? Because, as John Maxwell perfectly stated, "You can love people without leading them, but you cannot lead them without loving them." I know that her love for Andie has grown throughout the year as she has gotten to know her better and served her more, but what drove her leadership from the beginning was love.

I could tell you about how skilled Mrs. Moschetti is as a teacher. I could talk about how fun she is and about how she keeps the kids engaged. I could tell you about her knowledge and her ability to explain complex ideas in simple terms that third graders can understand. But that is not what made her Teacher of the Year. It is not what made her Andie's favorite. All of that skillset is assumed. As a parent, I assume she has the ability to teach. That's a given. When you're a leader, your people assume you have the knowledge and skill to do your job. That's a given.

What sets her apart is that she loves her students. That she partners with her students. And that she goes above and beyond. She cares.

That's why she is Teacher of the Year.

Think about it. Would you be Leader of the Year?
Overcoming self-interest, ego and apathy is not an easy task. We need to be aware that these stumbling blocks will never go away because they are human weaknesses and we are all susceptible to them on an ongoing basis, especially as our leadership roles grow. Leaders who remain vigilant at keeping these obstacles at bay will be well on their way to making a huge impact with their people, and engendering great commitment.

Partnership-based leadership is not a clever way of explaining leadership designed to sell books. It is an uncommon approach that is quickly catching on because of the results that it creates.

Approach & Result

I believe we choose the level of influence we have with our people based on the approach to leadership we choose to take. In my observation there are three distinct approaches to leadership and each derives a different result.

1. *Pretentious leaders* create contempt.
Pretentious leaders are driven by ego. Their focus is not on their people; it's on them. They choose style over function. When a leader is conceited, fake, disinterested or abrasive, they create feelings of resentment with their people. The lack of respect erodes trust and invites desires to undermine the leader's authority. It's easy to blame problems on your people and even

to fire people who seem to be a thorn in your side, but those fixes are never more than temporary. I want to be clear that pretentious leadership creates contempt.

2. *Positional leaders* create compliance.

When leaders rely on position or authority they are not truly leading. People don't follow titles, they follow people. If people follow you because they have to, it is influence bequeathed, not personally earned, and exercising it can be done lazily because following is not a choice. When people are forced or compelled to follow you, the most you will ever get out of them is compliance. And as Dondi Scumaci likes to say, "Compliance will never take you where commitment can go."

3. *Partner leaders* create commitment

Partner leaders understand that influence has to be earned. They build genuine relationships, add value, and join in collaboration with their people. That is what creates commitment. It is what every leader, salesperson, teacher, speaker, friend or mentor seeks. It is grounded in consistency of character. With this type of influence, no one is forced or compelled to follow you. Instead, they choose to follow you because they buy into you and find fulfillment and worth in your leadership.

Creating an atmosphere that makes people feel committed and engaged is no small challenge in our ever-changing economy. Time Magazine recently reported that less than half of American workers (45 percent) are satisfied with their jobs, the lowest percentage in a quarter of a century. A Gallup poll showed that an even higher percentage – 72 percent – are not engaged in their work, that they are "sleep walking through their day," and that the loss of productivity from actively disengaged employees costs the American economy $370 billion annually.

Engagement – commitment – is critical, and yet, an ACCOR study revealed that while 90 percent of leaders agreed that employee engagement equates to success, 75 percent admitted they had no engagement plan or strategy.

Summed up the Gallup report: "Leaders of great workplaces keep practicing to get better every day with their own teams. By displaying a little vulnerability and visibly working on improving themselves, they signal that such engagement is how one gets ahead."

What is Partnership Based Leadership?

The partnership based leadership approach is the leadership that works in today's world. I have shared this approach and watched it in action across the globe and through almost every industry. I don't claim to have invented it but I have coined the term because as I watch partner leaders in action I have been able to identify similar patterns, beliefs and behaviors that consistently produce results.

1. Partnership Based Leadership
Is The Way You View Your People

When you see your people as partners and not subordinates it changes your approach to leadership. It's not about top down directives but rather open conversation and buy-in. Your people feel heard and they feel valued.

Wayne Dyer taught: "When you change the way you look at things, the things you look at change." As leaders, when we shift our mindset to a partnership it impacts the way we communicate, the way we interact, the way we serve, and ultimately the influence we have with our people.

2. Partnership Based Leadership Is Built On Relationships
- **Partner leaders prioritize people over power.**
- **Partner leaders prioritize people over programs.**
- **Partner leaders prioritize people over policy, processes, and procedures.**

Le Roy H. Kurtz of General Motors once poignantly observed: "The fields of industry are strewed with the bones of those organizations whose leadership became infested with dry rot, who believed in taking instead of giving ... who didn't realize that the only assets that could not be replaced easily were the human ones." Partner leaders understand the value of their people and work hard to built genuine relationships that foster true commitment.

3. Partnership Based Leadership Is A Balanced Approach
I have taught audiences for years that leaders need to place their people first. That has led to debates with other leadership experts who argue that a leader needs to take care of their own needs first or they won't be in a position to lead effectively. The beauty of a balanced partnership approach is that both your people's needs and your own are met simultaneously. You create a win-win – that's how partnership works.

Empowering your people, allowing them to grow and succeed, does not make you anything less. In fact, it makes you more as a leader.

4. Partnership Based Leadership Fosters Natural Accountability – The Leader To The People And The People To The Leader
Too many leaders are guilty of hypocritical expectations – meaning they expect their people to behave one way and

exempt themselves from the same expectations. We just finished a large remodel of our house, so I had the good fortune of dealing with contractors for the last year. The truth is some were amazing and some were horrible. One of the horrible ones was the group that built the basketball court in the backyard. It seemed like a fairly easy project. They said it would take a few days. I gave them a 50 percent deposit and they got to work. After a couple of days the court was about 95 percent done and they disappeared. The only thing left to do was paint the logo we selected. I called, I sent them a text, I emailed, but I heard nothing. I didn't get a single response for over four months! Then one day they knocked on the door and said, "We are here to finish the court." They acted like nothing had ever happened. They completed the job and it looked great! As soon as they finished they asked me to pay them the rest of the money and I said, "I am happy to pay you but you took a four month window to finish the job, so I will take the same four month window to pay you." You can imagine how much they liked that.

This little experience is all too common in leadership. Think about the resentment and disrespect that comes from people who are given hypocritical expectations from their leader. It undermines influence and destroys leadership. Leadership is rooted in relationships and when there is a positive relationship, accountability occurs naturally. The leader is accountable to the people and the people are accountable to the leader.

My friend Sam Silverstein speaks to leaders around the world about the importance of being accountable. He states: "Growing up I heard over and over from my father, 'patience is a virtue.' I believe accountability is a virtue. Accountability is keeping your commitments to people. People are attracted to people who are honest, transparent and who care for other people. People are attracted to people who are accountable. Accountability doesn't stop with leadership, it starts there."

5. Partnership Based Leadership Is Driven By Passion

If the No. 1 thing we want is committed people, we need to start by looking in the mirror. Leaders who lack passion will have followers who lack commitment.

You've heard it said that the speed of the leader is the speed of the pack. That is especially true when we look at the attitude, the work ethic, the energy, and commitment of the leader. Pure passion will permeate your team, it will rub off on them, and it will inspire them.

The word passion originated at the time of Jesus Christ and was used to describe Christ's suffering. Knowing the etymology of the word gives us a unique insight into its meaning. Passion means being willing to suffer for something that you love. The kind of passion that inspires commitment shows up early, stays late, finds solutions, engages the team, and gets the job done.

6. Partnership Based Leadership Is Executed With Empathy

Great leaders understand that they are in the people business.

- **We need leaders who care more about people than they do numbers.**
- **We need leaders who focus on being interested, not interesting.**
- **We need leaders who use influence, not authority, to get things done.**
- **We need leaders who talk with people, not at people.**
- **We need leaders who truly care.**

If we understand that leadership begins and ends with people, then we understand the need to develop relationships, make connections, partner with our people, and show empathy.

Empathy is the ability to mutually *experience* the thoughts, emotions, and direct experience of others.

Empathy helps us lead individually not collectively. Empathy gives us unique insight into people. Empathy encourages leaders to understand the root cause behind poor performance. Empathy allows leaders to build and develop relationships with those they lead.

Empathy as a state of mind breeds more listening, more understanding and, therefore, more leadership!

When leadership is executed with empathy it changes lives.

Bob Gay, who serves on the board of the Anasazi Foundation, the renowned wilderness behavioral healthcare program based in Arizona that helps young people "discover and nurture the seeds of greatness that lie within," tells the story of a teenage girl enrolled in the program who was being transported to the starting point in the Arizona desert.

When they arrived at their destination and stopped the car, the first thing the girl did is jump out and start running. She looked back over her shoulder, expecting the leaders to yell at her to come back. Instead, they shouted, "Stop, we want to come with you."

Then they added, "If we're going to run, we need to go the way you're running."

The girl had no shoes on. She ran until her feet were bloody. She finally stopped running, turned to the leaders who had gone with her step for step, and said, "Thank you for being willing to experience my pain."

Partner leadership means empathizing with your people by striving to understand not only where they're coming from, but also where they're going.

7. Partnership Based Leadership Creates Transformation

There may be no better example of transformation and partner leadership than Dr. Nido Qubein, president of High Point University in High Point, North Carolina. The history of the private liberal arts school, founded in 1924, is of a small college without any major attention – until 2005. That is when Dr. Qubein was installed as the seventh president of the university and everything changed.

Nido Qubein grew up in the Middle East and came to the United States as a teenager and ended up attending High Point University. After graduating, he chose to stay in High Point and raise his family there although his career has taken him around the world. He is an award-winning speaker and has authored more than two-dozen books and audio programs worldwide. As a business leader, he is chairman of the Great Harvest Bread Company with 220 stores in 43 states. He serves on the boards of several national organizations, including the Fortune 500 financial company BB&T, La-Z-Boy Corporation, and Dots Stores, a chain of fashion boutiques with more than 400 locations across the country.

In 2005, High Point University was situated on 92 landlocked acres with a total undergraduate enrollment of 1,450. The university's operating budget was $35 million with a faculty of about 100 members. Then Dr. Qubein took over. The first thing he did after taking office was write the school a check in the amount of $1 million. It was the largest donation in the school's history. When asked why he was giving such a large amount, Nido said, "Because I am going to ask people to donate $1 million or more and I can't ask them to do something I wasn't willing to do." Within 24 hours he received more than ten checks for $1 million or more.

Nido's leadership has grown the school to over 300 acres and it's still expanding. He has overseen the construction of 72 new buildings and the renovation of many more to facilitate four new schools of study and the growing student body. Current enrollment is nearing 5,000.

He has raised money at an unprecedented rate. Ashley Furniture Industries chairman Ron Wanek donated $25 million in 2013 after a visit with HPU's president. Wanek's gift was the 10th contribution of $10 million or more Dr. Qubein accepted on behalf of the university. In the school's first 81 years, total donations amounted to $60 million. Since 2005, they have exceeded $275 million.

Having heard about this transformation, I arranged to visit the campus and spend the day with Nido to see firsthand his leadership in action. I toured the cleanest and most beautiful campus I have ever visited. It was immaculate! Everywhere we went students greeted the university president by waving and yelling, "Nido." He knows the name of every member of his staff and they know him and love him. Students and faculty are happy, devoted, engaged and committed. By applying the principles of partner leadership, Nido Qubein has created an atmosphere of trust and buy-in that has fostered incredible growth and fulfillment at a place few expected to see it happen.

The Seven Distinctions of Partner Leaders

In the following chapters you will learn what I call the Seven Distinctions of Partner Leaders.
These distinctions are:
1. **Partner leaders build genuine relationships.**
2. **Partner leaders know that value precedes influence.**

3. **Partner leaders generate buy-in.**
4. **Partner leaders master conversational leadership.**
5. **Partner leaders understand that motivation is important but it's also overrated.**
6. **Partner leaders recognize that culture eats strategy for lunch.**
7. **Partner leaders create leaders, not followers.**

The most relevant, effective, and influential leaders in today's world embody these seven distinctions. They are a set of beliefs, strategies, and practices that will help you to shape your leadership approach so that you garner the greatest commitment from your people.

TY'S *TAKEAWAY*

- **The old adage said: "Leadership is based on title, position or authority."**

- **In today's world: "Partnership Is The New Leadership."**

BUILD
GENUINE
RELATIONSHIPS

CHAPTER 2

PARTNER LEADERS BUILD GENUINE RELATIONSHIPS

One of my good friends, Paul Hineman, is the CFO of First Watch Restaurants, a breakfast, brunch, and lunch chain based in Florida.

I first met Paul when he was executive vice president of The National Restaurant Association, the largest food-service trade organization in the world. Because he loved the NRA so much, I was surprised when he told me he was leaving. When I asked why, without hesitation he said, "It's Ken Pendery, the CEO. Wait till you meet him and you will know what I mean."

Ken Pendery has been a key leader of First Watch Restaurants, Inc. for over 25 years. He has been instrumental in evolving the brand from a simple concept into a successful, multimillion-dollar enterprise. Ken is personable, sincere, and very approachable. An operator at heart, on most days he can be found in First Watch restaurants speaking with employees and greeting guests firsthand.

I have worked with the leadership in many companies across more than a dozen industries. As an outsider who comes in to train on leadership, it is fairly easy to get a feel for the culture, the commitment, and the connection between the leaders and those they lead. There are few companies I have come across where the CEO is as beloved and respected as at First Watch Restaurants. I found that Paul's admiration was a common theme throughout the company. Ken Pendery does a masterful job of building influential relationships with his people.

Over lunch I asked Ken what he viewed as his primary role as CEO and he said, "My job is to ensure that the company principles are upheld and the best way for me to do that is to be with my people, to know my people, to build great relationships with my people and to teach them what it means to be part of the First Watch family."

As a partner leader, Ken Pendery embodies The Seven Distinctions to a T – and he particularly shines at building influential relationships.

Following Ken's example and advice,
I want to propose five simple steps to building
genuine relationships with your people:
1. **Be With Your People**
2. **Get To Know Your People**
3. **Love Your People**
4. **Serve Your People**
5. **Lead Your People Individually**

1. Be With Your People

Spend time with the people you serve. Rub shoulders with them. Live where they live. Understand what their duties are, their responsibilities, their challenges. See things from their vantage point, at eye level.

The Marine Corps calls this "eyeball" leadership, where officers take time to walk in lockstep with those they are training and experience exactly what they are experiencing. They get in the trenches with them, literally. The result is cohesiveness, a closeness, a feeling of unity that couldn't be acquired any other way.

"Walk slowly through the crowd," advises John Maxwell. "Remember people's names, smile at everyone, and be quick to offer help. People don't care how much you know until they know how much you care."

Partner leaders understand the importance of being accessible, approachable and accountable.

Not surprisingly, when I bring this up when I'm speaking to leaders, the first pushback I get is "I'm so busy, how do I find time to build relationships with my people?"

My answer has two parts: accessibility and proactivity.

Do you, as a leader, make yourself accessible to those you lead? Do you eat lunch in the company cafeteria or are you always on your own? Do you have an open door for people to come and talk to you or are you closed off? When you are with your people do you make it feel as though you are approachable, that you are open to conversation, that you have time to ask them questions and answer their questions?

Making yourself accessible is step one. But to build genuine relationships you also have to be proactive about it. Leaders are busy. You have a lot on your plate, there are deadlines to be met, plans to be made. Prioritizing is vital, and prioritizing people should land at the top of the list. So you have to find your moments and plan for them. Maybe you have an opportunity to eat lunch once a week with one of your key leaders, maybe you can get to the office five minutes early and use that time to sit down with somebody on an individual basis. Leaders who are proactive about building relationships will be more successful and influential.

The next pushback from the leaders goes something like this: "If I lead 500 or 1,000 people, how do I build genuine relationships with all of them?"

That's a good question, and the short answer is: you can't. Research by a British anthropologist and Oxford professor named Robin Dunbar showed that any one person has the capacity to build and maintain meaningful relationships with 150 others. It's called the Dunbar Rule. Dunbar studied numerous social groups, from ancient hunter-gatherer tribes to modern companies of Marines, and found that plus or minus 150 is the magical number of close relationships we are naturally designed to manage. Attempting to maintain any more than that starts to break down social systems or effective hierarchy. No one person can single-handedly manage a large number of people and maintain a strong sense of trust, commitment and community.

If you're the leader of a thousand-person company, you have to build a hierarchy of leadership. Who are the key leaders and influencers you need to develop genuine relationships with who in turn will develop genuine relationships with the groups they lead? As a senior leader you must trust your mid-level leaders.

But if your organization has less than 150 people, maintaining and building relationships with each and every one of them is doable.

2. Get To Know Your People

Learn who they are, where they come from, where they want to go, what motivates them. Ask questions and listen. In conversations, focus on being interested, not interesting.

For a leader, the first step in forging strong and meaningful partnerships is making it about them, not you.

Don't Make Others Feel Small

I was once having a conversation with my assistant about another person. She paused for a moment and said, "Can I be honest?" I said, "Of course." Then she said, "Every time I interact with him, I feel like he has somewhere more important to be. He makes me feel like I don't matter, like he is having the conversation because he has to and not because he wants to and he is ready to move on as quickly as possible."

Have you ever felt that from someone else?

I'm sure we all have at one time or another. But the more pertinent question is, have you ever done that to someone else?

My friend Kevin Hall wrote a great book called *Aspire*. In the book he dissects the meaning of words and in the first chapter he introduces an Indian word – Genshai. Genshai means that you never treat another person in a manner to make them feel small. Leaders who practice genshai build people up, give people undivided attention and make them feel important.

I have noticed that one of the most common ways that we make other people feel small is when we don't give them time and attention. When we make others feel like they are not worth our time, we not only make them feel small but we erode our ability to influence and impact that person for good.

Once when I was speaking for the leadership team of First Watch Restaurants in Florida, we discussed the in-restaurant visits that the regional vice presidents make on a daily basis. One of the RVP's expressed a concern. He said, "How do we make each person feel important and spend the time when we have so much to get done. We don't have enough time in the day?"

My response was, "I know that you are busy and so am I. We all are. But don't make your issues become someone else's issues. The person you are sitting with doesn't need to know you are busy – it's not their issue, it's yours."

That may be harsh – but it's true.

When we give people time and attention, we make them feel important and we practice genshai.

When we act like we have somewhere more important to be and don't have time for them, we make other people feel small, which is the opposite of leadership.

Don't One-up

Another way we fail at getting to know our people is by one-upping them.

The common conversation:

You say: "I had the coolest experience last week. I was on a business trip in New York City meeting with a new client and they invited me to see Billy Joel in concert at Madison Square Garden! The seats were amazing and it was by far the best concert I have ever been to."

They reply: "Well you know the coolest concert I've ever been to…"

We have all had a version of this conversation or possibly hundreds of them. My question is – how does this make you feel about the other person?

When someone one-ups you in conversation it makes you shut down and close off. It doesn't leave you with a positive feeling toward that person and it definitely hurts all future interaction.

One-upping others in conversation is so common it's comical. Everyone who wants to make friends and gain influence with others needs to be aware of, and guard against, this natural likeability killer. For leaders, it is absolutely imperative.

The Rule of Two

I was speaking for Anthem Insurance in California and at one of the breaks a salesman named Joe asked if he could share an insight with me. Earlier that day I'd taught about focusing on *being interested, not interesting* and he said it reminded him of a rule he made for himself years ago called The Rule of Two.

Joe told me how he was called out early in his career for one-upping other people. It was affecting how he connected (or didn't connect) with others and it was undermining the influence he was trying to build. Joe decided to fix it and so he developed The Rule of Two. When someone says something about themselves, ask at least two questions before you say anything about yourself.

As an example: Your good friend says they like boating – they just bought an expensive boat and they go every weekend to the lake. You may be thinking, "What a bragger, oh really, well I…" But then you stop yourself and remember The Rule of Two. You respond: "I bet your family really enjoys that. How did you decide on the right boat for the family? And what was your favorite family moment at the lake this year?"

Wow, how that changed everything! You felt great about being truly interested in your friend. Your friend stopped his normal chatter and thought a minute about what was truly important about the boat and shared with you a personal moment with his family and experience. You made a connection that will not be forgotten, that could have been missed without using The Rule of Two.

Now think about doing that as a leader. Would you build stronger, long-lasting relationships by actually listening and responding from a place of interest? The next time you are heading down the road of one-upping, give Joe's idea a try. Use the principle of The Rule of Two!

3. Love Your People

My all time favorite leadership quote is from John Maxwell: "You can love people without leading them, but you cannot lead people without loving them."

When I was at High Point University, as I toured the campus with school president Dr. Nido Quebein, every student as we passed would ask, "Hey Nido, how are you?" Nido would respond warmly and ask in return how they were doing. When we walked into the basketball game that night, the entire student section chanted "Nido, Nido, Nido." It was like he was a rock star. The next morning when we talked in his office, he pointed out, "That's because I'm their friend." Then we had an interesting conversation about how partner leaders lead. We came to the conclusion that a partner leader is much like a parent. A parent is a friend but they're also respected and looked up to, and heard as a leader. That balance of being a friend to your people while maintaining your position of leadership is what partner leadership is all about.

Love for your people is the most important ingredient in the makeup of a leader. When people know that you care, that your concern is genuine, that you truly have their best interests at heart, they will respond with loyalty, trust and commitment.

Other leadership traits will vary, and sometimes vary wildly, but love is a constant.

Herb Kelleher, the founder of Southwest Airlines, tells a story about studying trial lawyers when he was a young attorney just getting started in San Antonio. He focused on the two most renowned litigators in the area. One of them never objected to anything, never raised his voice and was very gentle with witnesses and the jury. The other was loud, aggressive, forever raising objections. The only thing these lawyers had in common was they both seemed to win every case – and they genuinely cared about their clients. The takeaway for me was that there are many different paths to success, not just one. Fitting our own style and personality into any leadership role is essential. And they all can work, as long as caring and concern is included. It's why some leaders who might be a bit rough around the edges are still valued and accepted by their people, even though their interpersonal skills are not refined. When your people know that you care about them, they will care about you.

4. Serve Your People

Dwight D. Eisenhower once famously said: "You don't lead by hitting people over the head – that's assault, not leadership."

A soft touch, a willingness to listen and help is much more preferable – and effective.

As supreme commander of Allied Troops during World War II, Eisenhower led hundreds of thousands of men – 160,000 alone in the D-Day invasion – but still managed to make them think he knew them personally. His habit was to get out of his office whenever possible and walk and talk with men up and down the ranks, and he encouraged his officers to do the same.

"You must know every single one of your men," he taught. "It is not enough that you are the best soldier in that unit, that you are the strongest, the toughest, the most durable, the best equipped, technically – you must be their leader, their father, their mentor, even if you're half their age. You must understand their problems. You must keep them out of trouble, if they get in trouble, you must be the one who goes to their rescue."

In other words, serve those you lead.

Eisenhower embodied the precepts of servant leadership before that phrase was ever coined. That happened in 1970, when Robert K. Greenleaf founded the modern servant leadership movement with a memorable essay "The Servant as Leader," that inspired a generation of advocates and followers.

After spending 40 years studying management practices of U.S. businesses, Greenleaf's contention was that the authoritarian style of leadership routinely practiced – where the leader dictates what policies and procedures will be followed without any meaningful input from below – was a killer of both productivity and morale. Instead of being authoritative first, the leader should serve first.

"While traditional leadership generally involves the accumulation and exercise of power by one at the 'top of the pyramid,' servant leadership is different," he wrote. "The servant-leader shares power, puts the needs of others first and helps people develop and perform as highly as possible." His philosophy attracted many of the top thought leaders of our time, Ken Blanchard and Stephen R. Covey among them.

Serving reaps rewards far beyond the balance sheet and year-end reports. When you as a leader invest in your people, your people will invest in you.

5. Lead Your People Individually

I had a speech in Connecticut speaking for a leadership group at The Hartford. Since it was two hours away from New York City, I decided to take my oldest daughter, Andie, and make a trip out of it. We had a blast! We explored the city from the 9/11 Memorial to Central Park. We saw Matilda on Broadway and even made a long visit to The American Girl Doll store. In May, I took my son Tanner on a fishing trip to Idaho. We camped out, we got rained on, we caught trout and cooked it, and we even caught a 150-pound sturgeon. It was a totally different experience but an amazing bonding experience all the same.

Each month we do a lot of things as a family, but my wife, Sarah, and I also do individual dates with our kids.

The reason we do this is because we believe leadership is individual.

You don't lead a group of people, you lead individual people who make up a group. That is why it is important for leaders to find individual time with their people. Time to have one-on-one conversation. Time to get to know their needs, fears, strengths and goals. Time to understand what drives each individual.

Great leaders not only make individual time for their people, but understand that the object is to build up, not tear down. Emphasizing the positive is paramount.

Let me tell you what I mean by that. I have four kids. I have a 9-year-old, a 6-year-old, a 4-year-old and an almost 2-year-old, and as a parent I think I do an OK job but I always want to do better. I always want to learn. I want to look at what other parents are doing. I want to read about parenting. I want to become as good a parent as I possibly can. One of the studies I read recently talked about how anytime you chastise or criticize a child, you want to praise them five times to make up for that, to balance the emotions of the child. Because, in essence, this article was saying negative weighs five times more than positive.

As an example, let's say you're walking down the street and

you find a $20 bill. You look around, there's nobody there. It is a free $20 bill and it's just sitting there. There is a certain amount of oxytocin released in your brain that is a positive brain chemical, produced by a positive experience. Now let's say you jump in the car and you're driving along and you decide to roll the window down and that $20 bill is sitting on the passenger seat and the wind comes up and blows it out the window. You can't believe it, you freak out, because you just lost $20! It's the same $20 you just found, but here's what happens: the amount of cortisol released in your brain when you lose the bill is actually five times more than the amount of oxytocin released when you found it. Why? Negative weighs five times more than positive.

If you and I want to manage the emotional relationships we have with our people, we need to praise, encourage and have positive experiences with them five times more than we criticize and have negative experiences. If we have to correct, it's part of leadership, it happens. But we need to make up for it. We need to manage the emotional relationship by keeping a positive balance. We need to have five positive experiences for every one negative experience. If you can effectively manage the emotional relationships with your people, it's going to change the equation. They are going to come away feeling positive about you, positive about their leadership, and positive about the relationship.

In my book, *The Power of Influence,* I talk about the Platinum Rule. It is a step above the Golden Rule. The Golden Rule focuses on treating others the way you want to be treated, but the Platinum Rule is to treat others the way they want to be treated. When we individualize our approach to leadership we recognize each person as separate and distinct, with specific needs and wants. Knowing that allows us to partner and lead in a truly effective manner. It requires more investment from a leader to spend meaningful time with your people, to get to really know and serve them, and lead each person individually. But the investment will pay off. Your people will be more committed and your influence and impact will expand exponentially.

TY'S *TAKEAWAY*

- **The old adage said: "It's lonely at the top."**

- **In today's world: "Business is all about relationships."**

CHAPTER 3

PARTNER LEADERS KNOW THAT VALUE PRECEDES INFLUENCE

In the 1940s a small boutique financial services firm was just beginning to finally see a bit of success. They had started out when two people came together with the hopes to create something great. They decided at this point to add someone to their marketing department. They found a guy named Charles Engle – a journalist by background who at the time was working as an editor of a magazine. He had just started to have some experience in advertising and marketing, and found that he loved that much more than he loved journalism. So when this job opportunity came up he was the perfect fit for them. He did not have much experience and they did not have much money – perfect fit.

He began his job and started to look at what they were doing when it came to marketing. At that time you have to remember how financial services worked – stock brokers knew things that most of the rest of the world did not. That's how they liked it. That was by design. They didn't want people to understand the stock market; they wanted to be the sole owners of that information. They wanted to be the experts so people had to come to them.

Most of the ads that were run at the time were pretty simple, a couple hundred words – things like "Come to us if you want to make money. We will help you invest in the stock market." Just a straightforward pitch. As he looked at the marketplace, Charles Engle asked, "How can we add value to our customers? What can we give them in this ad?"

He went to his bosses and said, "Look, what if we shared valuable information? What if we taught people about the stock market?" His bosses didn't get it and thought he was crazy. "Why would we want to do that?" they asked. His response, "If we give them value, if we invest in them – then they will want to invest in us." Charles wanted to show his bosses what he meant so he wrote up an ad. They read it and asked, "There is some really good information here, are we giving away too much?" His reply, "the more you give away, the more they are going to want." They decided to run the ad.

The ad was 6,500 words. That's like an eBook today – a huge ad. Within a week that ad produced 3,000 leads. This was long before the connected world we live in today, where responding is a hyperlink click on your iPhone. This was a time when you'd read it in the newspaper, cut out the form, fill it out, put it in an envelope, put a stamp on it, take it to the post office, and send it in – that's the kind of lead that was. They got 3,000 of those in a week! Over the next five years that ad produced over five million leads and turned that little boutique financial services firm into the company you and I know as Merrill Lynch.

That happened because Charles Engle understood that **value precedes influence.**

The Struggle

When I was 21 years old my brother Scott and I started a business together in direct sales. I would love to say that it took off like a rocket but that isn't true. Although we eventually had great success, I initially struggled to get people to buy into me, buy from me, and choose to do business with me. I remember reading several self-development and business books that kept referring to The Golden Rule of Business: People Do Business With People They Know, Like & Trust.

I remember thinking, "That's not true. People seem to know me, like me and trust me, and yet they won't do business with me! What am I missing?" One day I was sharing this concern with a mentor and he simply asked, "Ty, what value do you bring to people?"

"What do you mean?" I replied. Then he explained, "Value precedes influence. In fact, it is adding value that makes you influential. When you add value to someone's life, they want more from you. They want you around. They want to do business with you. They buy into you." And then he hit me between the eyes, "Your problem is not getting people to know you, like you or trust you. Your problem is communicating the value you bring. Until you learn to do that you will never have the influence you want."

What he was telling me is that the real Golden Rule of Business is actually: People Do Business With People They Know, Like, Trust & **Value.** If there was ever a recipe for leadership, that is it.

So I asked my mentor, "What should I do? I don't know what I am doing wrong in my approach. I'll do anything, just tell me what to do."

He suggested I go back and talk to the last five people who told me no and ask them what I was doing wrong. He said,

"Have a genuine conversation. Be humble and honest. Tell them that you want to be better and you would love it if they would tell you how you could be better or why they chose not to do business with you."

My initial reaction was, "I will do anything but that!" But I consented and nervously went to talk to the last five people who told me no. It was one of the most eye opening experiences I have ever had. It was amazing. They were honest and sincere and helped me to see some blind spots I didn't know existed.

Although they mentioned many things I could do better, all five said their biggest concern was my age. At 21 years old they just didn't see what I had to share with them that was worth listening to.

The truth is the thought had never crossed my mind. I was just young enough and cocky enough that I didn't realize how major of a concern it was for the more experienced, more successful people I was talking to.

With this newfound knowledge I returned to my mentor and said, "It is because of my age." He quickly replied, " I know." I said, "Well, if you knew, why did you have me go back and talk to them?" He said, "You had to hear it for yourself." And he was right.

So I asked, "What do I do."

He said, "I don't know."

"I don't know! What do you mean? I am not going to wait until I am 40 to start in business – what do I do?"

He said, "What did other young entrepreneurs do? What did Bill Gates do? What did Steve Jobs do?"

Right when he said Bill Gates, I had an idea. It was an idea that turned into a way for me to communicate my value and to lend me credibility.

After that, when I sat down with people I sensed might have a bias against me because of my youth, I'd start off by saying, "You know, it's interesting as I'm talking to you because I know some people look at me and they think what does this guy know about business? He's young, he's 21. He really doesn't have a ton of experience. But you know, I kind of feel like a young Bill Gates." When I put it that way, most of the time they would smile and then I'd say, "What I mean is, you know, Bill Gates was 19 years old when he started Microsoft. He dropped out of college and he had this vision, he told everyone that he was going to take computers, which were the size of refrigerators, and he was going to put one in every house in the world. People probably thought he was nuts. Who was this young, naïve entrepreneur?"

Then I'd continue: "Now, I'm not saying that I'm going to change the world, and I'm not saying that I'm going to make as much money as Bill Gates. What I am saying is that I have something here and I know where I'm going with this, and I want you to really sit down and take a look at it. Are you willing to do that?"

That story communicated value in a way that caused people to take me seriously and soon people began to listen. With a lot of hard work, my brother and I were able to grow our business to over $20 million in annual revenue while still in our twenties.

Value Precedes Influence.

"I'll Work For Free"

My friend Scott Schwerdt is president of The Americas Region for Nu Skin Enterprises, a multi-billion dollar company based in Provo, Utah. Scott has been with Nu Skin for more that 25 years and is an adored leader and employee. Before starting with Nu Skin more than two decades ago, Scott worked for the CIA. He loved what he did but it wasn't conducive to the young family he and his wife were starting. So Scott left the CIA and moved to Provo to be near family.

He began to look for work and interviewed with Steve Lund, the co-founder of a new company called Nu Skin. Scott bought into Steve's vision and saw great potential with the company and Steve also connected with Scott and thought he would be great to add to the team. But as is the case with many young companies, funds were tight and they didn't have the money to pay Scott what he was asking. Steve called Scott to tell him the unfortunate news. He said, "Scott, we would love to have you as part of the team but we simply can't afford you right now. I am sorry."

Scott's reply was probably shocking: "Well then I'll work for free to start."

And that is what he did. He showed up because he believed in the company and knew he could help.

He did help, and continues to help. Over a quarter of a century the company has expanded by leaps and bounds and Scott has been part of the growth and had opportunities to grow in position as well. He has gone from a customer service manager to account manager to eventually president of one of the seven areas of the world for the company.

I am not implying in any way that Scott does not deserve the promotions he has been given – he has earned every position and bonus. But I want you to put yourself in the owner's shoes – would you not feel absolute loyalty to someone who came to work for you for free?

The idea that value precedes influence is the opposite mentality of the instant gratification, give-it-to-me-now world.

The rampant attitude is, "If you pay me more, I will work harder." "If you give me the promotion then I will put in the extra hours."That actually has it backwards. You do whatever "that" is well, dependably, for a long time, and THEN they pay you more because you have earned it. True leaders know that when they add value they grow their influence. They approach a situation with an attitude of service and giving. They think, "What can I give?" instead of "What do I get?"

The first time I ever met Dr. Stephen Covey (famed author of *The Seven Habits of Highly Effective People*) he taught me that most people go through life thinking that it is about achievement, but when we learn what life is really about, we realize it is about contribution. There is a big difference.

Astute leaders understand that learning to focus on contribution and not achievement, on others and not yourself, provides the mindset to know that value precedes influence.

20 Ways Leaders Add Value

I was recently speaking to a group of managers about this idea that value precedes influence. One of the managers raised his hand and said, "Can you give me a list of 20 ways I can add value as a leader?"

Here is my list:
1. **Spend one-on-one time with your people.**
2. **Recognize publicly.**
3. **Compliment others sincerely.**
4. **When mistakes are made be curious, not critical.**
5. **Buy lunch.**
6. **Give credit to the team.**

7. **Allow others opportunities to lead the meeting, give the presentation, take the lead or be in the limelight.**
8. **Know your people's names, hobbies, likes, etc.**
9. **Constantly be learning.**
10. **Share your knowledge.**
11. **Connect people who could benefit each other.**
12. **Share books/articles that would be beneficial.**
13. **Be caring enough to have candid conversations.**
14. **Ask better questions.**
15. **Write a handwritten note.**
16. **Support someone's project or initiative.**
17. **Listen more, talk less.**
18. **Reach out just because.**
19. **Go out of your way to promote the agenda of others.**
20. **Remember birthdays.**

Three Questions To Ask Yourself

In a conversation on adding value, *New York Times* bestselling author Brendan Burchard proposed three questions we should ask ourselves.

As you finish a project, contribute to the team or look for ways to add value as a partner leader, I want you to ask yourself these three questions on a regular basis. I personally put them on a sticky note on my computer as I was writing this book because I want the content to add enormous value. Answering all three in the affirmative will accomplish that goal.

Question 1: Is what I am creating/contributing distinct?

Is your contribution different in a significant way? Is it adding value in a way that no one else has done? Does it stand out? Does it look and feel esthetically unique? Is it something that

will impress people because it is coming from an angle that others haven't thought of?
• It's not crazy or out there, but it is distinct and stands out.

Question 2: Is this my most excellent contribution?

Did you just throw it together or did you do a good job? Did you put in the time to prepare and give it your best effort? Did you make it look amazing and professional? Did you ask people questions in the preparation to make sure you added relevant value? Did you solicit sufficient feedback so that you are confident it will be well received?
• When we strive for excellence, we put in the effort that pays off.

Question 3: Is there heart in here?

Did you approach it with a service mindset? Are you striving to help others or to make yourself look great? Is there emotion in this thing you have contributed? Will people feel your passion?
• Part of the way we add value as leaders is to bring the flare, the inspiration, and the vibrancy that people are looking for.

President or Professor?

At High Point University there are several ways that Dr. Nido Qubein has continued to add value. In his leadership role he is working to grow his influence with the teachers and staff, the students, their parents, the alumni, potential donors, and the surrounding community.

One of the ways he has added value is by creating a lecture series that brings in thought leaders, world leaders, and celebrities. These lectures that have featured Malcolm Gladwell, Steve Wozniak, Colin Powell, and others are available to students and staff – but also to the community. They are a popular event in the small town of High Point and one of the important ways he has added value.

Another unique way Nido has made an impact and added value is by teaching a life skills class to all incoming freshman. It is a required class that teaches the basics of success. He covers everything from how to live on your own to how to thrive in your college career. Nido told me, "I wanted a chance to interact with all of our incoming freshman, for me to get to know them and them to get to know me. I wanted to set the tone for their success at High Point, inspire them and give them skills to be successful while they are here."

Nido also teaches a class for all seniors before they graduate. This class focuses on the intangible skills they will need to be successful in their careers and in life. He talks to them about being a lifelong learner, how to be a leader and how to keep your priorities in place. When I asked about this class he simply said, "High Point is not about getting a degree, it is about becoming a successful person. That is what we do and I want to make sure I do my part to make that happen."

It is no wonder to me that Nido is a beloved university president. No ivory tower for him. He is constantly giving of his wisdom, his experience, and his creativity.

When a leader adds value they grow their influence.

TY'S *TAKEAWAY*

- **The old adage said, "Title gives you the right to be heard."**

- **In today's world, "Value gives you the right to be heard."**

CHAPTER 4

PARTNER LEADERS GENERATE BUY-IN

Through the course of history, numerous books have been written about how a leader's vision is what creates buy-in. The word vision comes from the Old German word "vissen" which means: *I Know What I See*. As a leader, if you are clear about your vision and display confidence in its application – if you know what you see and are sure of where you're going – others will "catch your vision" and you will attract support, trust, cooperation and approval from your people.

One of my favorite historical examples of confidence and ability to inspire followers with a clear vision is the story of Joan of Arc. Joan was born an ordinary child in a little French village in 1412. As a girl growing up, history records that she was healthy and happy, possessing a merry disposition.

At this time, France was suffering through its Hundred Years War with England. France had lost nearly every battle. Eight thousand Englishmen had wiped out sixty thousand Frenchmen at Agincourt. The French were hurting and their courage and confidence were lost. They had become, in essence, nothing more than a British province.

It was then, at the age of thirteen, that Joan began to feel that she would be God's instrument in setting France free. And while she questioned it at first, she eventually accepted her calling with full confidence, saying,"If it is commanded, I will go. I know that France will rise again, for God has ordained her to be free."

Joan, now seventeen, went to see the Dauphin, who was the uncrowned heir to the throne. The Dauphin said to her, "Tell me who you are?" Joan's reply was, "I am called Joan the Maid. I am sent to say to you that the king of heaven wills that you should give me men-at-arms and set me at my appointed work. For I will raise the siege of Orleans and break the British Power." Joan then said to the Dauphin, "Be not afraid, God has sent me to save you."

Joan's confidence and sincerity won the confidence of the Dauphin who gave her command of the French Armies. In a public proclamation the Dauphin said, "Know all men, that the most illustrious Charles, by the grace of God, King of France, is pleased to confer upon his well-beloved servant Joan of Arc, called the Maid, the title, emoluments, and authorities of General-in-Chief of the armies of France."

Louis Kossuth said, "Since the writing of human history began, Joan of Arc is the only person of either sex who has ever held supreme command of the military forces of a great nation at age 17."

She had a suit of armor made for her at Tours. She rode a white horse and carried the sacred sword of St. Catherine. She led the men to Orleans with supreme confidence that success would be theirs.

With what seemed to be an impossible task, Joan said to one of her generals, "I will lead the men over the wall." The general replied, "Not a man will follow you." Joan said, "I will not look back to see whether anyone is following or not."

The soldiers did follow their courageous leader and on May 8, 1430, she broke the siege at Orleans. This day is still celebrated as Joan of Arc Day. It is the day she saved France. Then, she and her troops marched to Rheims and crowned the Dauphin as king.

The vision and confidence of Joan of Arc created a buy-in by the French soldiers that was all-in. They wanted what she wanted, and they wanted it just as badly as she did. The result was a resounding success that reverberates nearly six hundred years later.

Everyone was united in the cause. That is the critical component for true buy-in. Without it, no matter how grand the plan, a leader will go into battle without followers.

Who Knew Changing A Name Was So Hard

I am a member of The National Speakers Association. It is a fantastic organization that has benefited my career and me greatly. At the 2014 national convention in San Diego, the association leadership introduced a rebranding for the association that included a new name. Instead of being known as The National Speakers Association we would now be called "Platform." The prep work for this name-change was incredible. The leaders had spent considerable time discussing it and done some amazing research. The presentation to introduce it at the convention was impeccable (what else would you expect from The National Speakers Association?).

Yet even with all that in place – the membership was not on board. The name-change topic quickly became a virtual lightning rod as blogs were written, videos and comments were shared online, and a social media frenzy erupted. In the court of majority opinion, "Platform" was clearly not winning. The leadership handled the situation with poise and cool heads and eventually decided to ditch the new name and re-evaluate the rebranding process.

For now we stay The National Speakers Association.

So what was the problem?

Was it the need? No – the research backed up the decision to rebrand.

Was it the name? No – many people loved the name.

Was it the presentation? No – it was really well done.

Why, then, didn't it work?

I think what was missed one of the key leadership lessons that is so easy to overlook. And it's something that in today's world is an absolute must.

Today, we need to understand that **people support what they help create.**

You see, sitting in that room with about 2,000 speakers, when the name change was introduced, there were only about a dozen people who knew what was coming. I'm fairly involved in the association. I was in a mastermind group at the time, with the president elect, a past national president and a member of the national board. I was the immediate past president of the Mountain West Chapter and I'm on a national committee. I'd never heard about this. I think most people were pretty blindsided by it.

The membership was not included in the process and they wouldn't support what they didn't create. The result wasn't approval; it was a revolt.

Our world has changed, and rapidly. Fifteen years ago, if you wanted your voice to be heard, you pretty much only believed it was heard if you held a position of leadership. Social media has changed all that and I don't mean just because people have Facebook or Twitter or LinkedIn where they can go and voice their opinion. It has changed the psyche of our world. It has caused everyone to feel like his or her voice should be heard. Regardless of where people are in your organization, they mentally believe that their voice and their opinion matters. As a result, our top-down directives don't work the same way they used to. We can't just throw things at people and expect them to jump on it, to run with it, and go for it. We need to understand that now more than ever. People support what they help create.

Sharing this example is not an attack on the board of NSA or anyone involved in this process. I am good friends with many people on the national board and respect their ideas and leadership a great deal. But I believe there was a major mistake made when they didn't involve the membership in the process. They never effectively got buy-in.

One of the important tenets of leadership and influence is co-creation. When people create it – they support it.

So how do we become better at involving our people? I am starting to see examples of it in many creative ways. I recently worked with a restaurant chain that used social media and feedback from their customers to shape their menu. Brilliant! At a conference where I was invited to speak, the company surveyed the attendees ahead of time to help create the conference theme and content, The audience was engaged and energetic. Why? Because it truly was *their* conference.

As influencers and leaders it may be more than involving our team. We may need to create buy-in and co-creation with our customers, vendors, managers, colleagues, or within our industry.

There are numerous great examples of how leaders facilitate co-creation – but let's remember the lesson from NSA: people support what they create.

It Takes Too Long

Getting everyone's input, creating universal buy-in, all-for-one-and-one-for-all: it all looks great on paper, but in practicality it doesn't make sense! That's the common retort I hear from managers. Including everyone simply takes too long.

The answer: it does take longer, but it's worth it. The time spent on the front end will be long lasting on the back end. The results are what matter, and the consequences of buy-in through team building will be motivated people who will take ownership and you will have the level of commitment you desire. As you start to look at the culture in your organization, remember that leaders don't create cultures for people; they create cultures with people.

In his book, *Leaders Eat Last: Why Some Teams Pull Together and Others Don't,* Simon Sinek writes:

"The true price of leadership is the willingness to place the needs of others above your own. Great leaders truly care about those they are privileged to lead and understand that the true cost of the leadership privilege comes at the expense of self-interest … Let us all be the leaders we wish we had."

Every leader and influencer needs to learn how to facilitate the co-creation process. When people are heard they will be helpful. When people are involved they are empowered. When people collaborate they will be committed.

Who cares who gets the credit

One reason leaders still take a top down approach is because they want the credit for the plan/strategy/approach. It's only natural to seek recognition but it's limiting and debilitating to your effectiveness.

Leadership comes in all shapes and sizes and examples of exceptional leadership are often found in the most unexpected of places.

I was watching the television show "The Voice" when a band called "Great Big World" performed their song, "Say Something." Music has a special way to move us by completely being relatable, heartfelt, happy, sad and sometimes just entertaining. It touches us and makes us feel something. That's what happened when Christina Aguilera heard "Say Something." She loved it and wanted to know everything about the artists and songwriters. The short story is this – she tracked down "Great Big World" and proposed a collaboration. As one of the judges on "The Voice" she offered to help get the song, and the group, on the show.

Most people view Christina as one of the most talented vocalist of our time, but also as a "Diva." You are now thinking why are we having this discussion? It's because Christina Aguilera gave her all for this song without needing top billing or recognition. She didn't ask for a solo part or do anything to stand out – she simply harmonized with "Great Big World" when they performed their song. She even dressed down so as to not draw attention to herself. In the end, "Great Big World" got noticed by more people, and a larger audience heard, and was moved by, their song.

Christina Aguilera demonstrated the type of leader who does not need to take credit. Her effort was certainly undeniable but she highlighted the original artists that gave birth to this song, not her own talents or agenda.

Andrew Carnegie once said, "No man will make a great leader who wants to do it all himself or get all the credit for doing it." Harry S. Truman echoed that when he stated, "It is amazing what you can accomplish if you do not care who gets the credit."

Ask yourself: do you want your team to succeed as much as you want yourself to succeed? Or are you the type of leader who believes that partnership with the team will create success for everyone, and at a level far greater than the sum of the individual parts?

The Commitment Scale - The Four D's

So how do you get your team involved? How do you attain full commitment from your people? One good way is to remember the four D's that make up the commitment scale. As a leader, you can use these steps to help your people to progress to a level of full buy-in and complete commitment.

These are the four levels:
Distraction. Decision. Discipline. Devotion

Distraction
People get distracted. It's a human thing. They have an idea what they want and where they want to go, but every single shiny object that comes along diverts them from realizing their goal. How many people do you know who want to lose a few pounds and get more fit, but when it comes to exercise, they get sidetracked by a phone call, or a trip to the store, or maybe a sudden urge to organize their office? It's just easier to seek the path of least resistance.

Distractions are the comfort zone. The bright shiny object is simply exciting, energizing, it takes us away from being bored. It also takes us away from our goals.

Leaders understand that distractions are the enemy. Getting your people to focus on the task at hand, and stay focused, is the first step to realizing full commitment.

Decision

The word "decision" in Latin means to cut off all other options. Making a decision can be scary. When we decide on a course of action, that means change and all change requires some level of discomfort. We are unsure of the outcome; we're forced out of our comfort zone, and we're accountable for the result. Making a decision is as much emotional as it is intellectual. It requires a high level of self-confidence.

Partner leaders understand this and ensure that decision-making is a collaborative effort. That no one is alone. They realize that their people will feel confident and want to make decisions when they know that decision-making is highly encouraged and rewarded, and that they are not going to be hung out to dry it the outcome isn't perfect.

Discipline

Making a decision opens the door to possibility; managing the decision turns it into reality. It is an old saying, "Integrity is following through on a decision long after the emotions felt when making the decision have passed." I call that discipline.

All of us can relate to losing the excitement and emotion of a decision that has been made. Oftentimes, the follow-through becomes tedious or challenging and we forget why we made the decision in the first place. Discipline requires us to not let that happen, to always keep sight of our goals, and to revisit the emotions that created them on a regular basis.

Partner leaders recognize that consistency and stick-to-it-iveness are the key ingredients of discipline and that these components are critical to the success and contentment of everyone involved.

Devotion

The pinnacle of the commitment scale is devotion. Eliminating distractions, making decisions, and exercising diligent discipline are all important steps, but full commitment requires devotion. As the great tenor Luciano Pavarotti said, "People think I am disciplined. It's not discipline. It is devotion. There is a great difference."

When you are devoted, you are driven by a cause, you are a person on a mission. You are not just *excited* about your decision; you are *passionate* about it. Devotion is felt internally, yet is externally obvious to everyone. Devotion is founded in purpose and without it full and complete commitment is not possible.

Partner leaders appreciate that people who are disciplined are effective, but people who are devoted are unstoppable.

Where are your people on the commitment scale? Do they feel the same ownership that you do? When they reach that point – when what you're doing matters to everyone on the team, regardless of their assignment – you will have true buy-in and commitment.

TY'S *TAKEAWAY*

- **The old adage said, "Leaders lay out the vision and expect others to jump on board."**

- **In today's world, "People support what they help create."**

CHAPTER 5

PARTNER LEADERS MASTER CONVERSATIONAL LEADERSHIP

Do you think your ability to communicate will make you or break you in business?

I have asked this question of audiences around the world and the response is always 100% affirmative. No one disputes that the ability to effectively communicate opens doors and establishes solid relationships.

As leaders, we are in the people business and so our communication is the currency of our business. To strengthen the value of that currency we need to focus not only on what we communicate, but how.

Typically, when leaders think about how they talk to their people, these are the questions they ask themselves: Am I articulate? In my emails, speeches, and staff meetings do I present a clear message? Am I confident and persuasive? Do people buy into me?

All these are good questions, but they focus on the leader's side of the dialogue. To be truly effective as a partner leader, you need to look at the other side. You need to understand and master the art of conversational leadership.

It's not about talking at your people – it's about talking *with* your people.

I have taught this idea for the last couple of years to leaders around the world. It is a concept that I developed from my own experiences in leadership and from working with thousands of leaders. I thought I might have coined a new term for a new kind of communication strategy. But as I began to write this chapter I Googled "conversational leadership" and realized that others have also grasped the concept and the name.

Executive coach and leadership consultant Craig Fleck described conversational leadership this way:

"Conversational leadership emphasizes keen attention, self-discipline, and a certain kind of artistry in engaging and communicating with others. Conversational leadership does not mean indulging in endless talking but rather identifying and engaging with the crucial and often courageous exchanges that facilitate meaningful change.

"It begins with a leader understanding that one of their critical functions in shaping and evolving an organization is to consciously address the essential conversations which form how people think and act. Many of these conversations go unspoken in public settings, remaining unaddressed because they often reveal the conflicts or tensions that lie below the surface, bringing controversy and disagreement in their wake. It takes courage for a leader to step into this territory, as it asks them to let go of control and open up to the input and differences of others."

"The traditional approach is for the leader to figure out what is right, and then persuade others to do it. Alternatively, engaging in conversational leadership is to "invite what you do not expect," bringing you to the frontier of what is emerging in your organization and asking you to turn into it, rather than away from it."

Harvard Professors Boris Groysberg and Michael Sind write about conversational leadership in their book *Talk Inc.* They refer to the Four I's that make for effective communication: Intimacy, Interactivity, Inclusion, and Intentionality. Leaders should connect emotionally when they converse with their people, they should take care to ensure the dialogue goes back and forth, they should cede enough control to stimulate a free exchange of ideas, and they should recognize the need to keep everyone together regarding the company's agenda and goals.

The authors note that establishing a culture of conversation won't always mean hitting each of the four "I's," but stress that these elements "tend to reinforce each other" to create a highly iterative process in which good ideas have a chance not only to be heard but to be developed.

The Three-Step Process

Leaders who adopt the style of conversational leadership create dialogue, trust, and collaboration within their organization. As their people feel heard, they become engaged, energized, and committed. Being a part of the conversation is so much more energizing than being a silent partner.

So how to we get there? How do we, as leaders, develop the skill of talking conversationally with our people?

The process can be broken down into three steps.
1. **Take The Right Approach**
2. **Create Balance**
3. **Make a Connection**

As we dissect each step, I want to invite you to read with an open mind and an honest assessment of how you are communicating and leading your people currently.

STEP ONE. TAKE THE RIGHT APPROACH
The way we approach communication decides our leadership style. Let me ask you several questions:
- **Do your people feel comfortable with you?**
- **Do they feel heard?**
- **Do you ask questions and really listen?**
- **In your team meetings are you doing most of the talking?**

If your answer to the all these questions is "yes," then you're definitely on the right track. If any of you answers are "no," then you've identified areas you could work on.

If we want commitment and engagement from our people, our purpose should be to create an active exchange of thoughts, concerns, objections, and ideas. When your people – your partners – feel heard, valued, and appreciated, they will reciprocate by listening and valuing what you share as well.

I believe that every leader chooses the level of influence they have based on the approach to leadership that they take.

Those who choose to lead based on title and position and communicate with an authoritative, top-heavy style, will realize influence that is only situational and small. Some would argue that your influence would be non-existent.

On the other hand, if you choose to lead based on relationships and by adding value, your communication will be collaborative and all encompassing – and your influence will be lasting and unlimited.

Leaders today who choose to communicate conversationally know the importance of the three A's: Accessibility, Approachability, and Authenticity.

Accessibility: As a leader are you accessible to your people? Do you take the time to be with them and make yourself available? If you want to build genuine relationships, you need to spend time with your people, get to know them and grow to love them. That requires more effort on your part – but that is the cost of leadership.

Approachability: Do your people feel like they can come to you with concerns or mistakes? Are you approachable? A lot of this has to do with the way that you carry yourself and the way you communicate. What tone do you use when you speak? What does your body language say? When someone shares a mistake are you curious or are you critical? Do you come across as guarded and judgmental or are you approachable?

Authenticity: People don't want perfect leaders – they want authentic leaders. They want you to be honest. They want you to not take yourself too seriously. They want you to share more experience and less opinion. They want to relate to you and connect with you. I believe our world is screaming for authenticity – especially in leadership.

Your communication style is your choice and in the end will produce results based on your ability to connect with your people. Is what you are currently doing creating the results to lead you to the success you are ultimately looking for? Or is it time to try a different approach?

STEP TWO. CREATE BALANCE

Communication is an art, and like any great art it requires a delicate balance.

There are three specific balances that I want to suggest.

1. **Care & Candor**
2. **Conversational versus Condescending**
3. **Curious versus Critical**

Care & Candor

A lot of management groups ask me to talk about year-end reviews and my answer is always the same: I don't believe in year-end reviews. That's because the candid conversations we want to have on a regular basis with our people, and that are so crucial to making progress and achieving success, need to be spontaneous and happen in the moment.

Creating an atmosphere conducive to having these frank talks in a way that is productive and as painless as possible lies at the heart of conversational leadership. People tend to respond well to constructive criticism when they feel valued and a part of the conversation.

In his book, *The 5 Levels of Leadership,* John Maxwell states, "If you care about people, treat them with respect, and build positive relationships with them, you actually have more numerous opportunities to speak candidly and have hard conversations with them that will help them to grow and perform better."

Partner leaders understand that caring and candor are equally important. Writes Maxwell: "Care without candor creates dysfunctional relationships. Candor without care creates distant relationships. But care balanced with candor creates developing relationships. Caring for others demonstrates that you value them. However, if you want to help them get better, you have to be honest about where they need to improve. That shows that you value the person's potential. That requires candor."

Maxwell also points out that being candid is a two-way street: "If you want to be an effective leader, you must allow the people you work with to be candid with you. You must solicit feedback. And you must be mature and secure enough to take in people's criticism without defensiveness and learn from it."

Winston Churchill said, "Criticism may not be agreeable, but it is necessary. It fulfills the same function as pain in the human body. It calls attention to an unhealthy state of things." Partner leaders know how to deliver the message encased in caring.

Conversational versus Condescending

Too many leaders talk down to their people. They belittle them and in many cases, because of the "yes sir" mentality of top-down conversation, they don't even realize they do it.

Do you talk at your people or do you talk with your people?

One way of answering that question is by asking yourself another question: Do you give commands or extend invitations?

A command would sound like this:
"You need to do this ..."

An invitation would sound like this:
"We need to be better, let's ..."

The only difference between the command and the invitation above is to change the vocabulary to collective. Using we, us, or let's makes the exchange feel like a partnership. We are in it together.

Here's another example of command versus invitation:
Command: "Stacy – you are going to take the lead on the project and it needs to be completed by Monday."
Invitation: "Stacy – will you head up the project? It is important and needs to be completed by Monday."

Beyond using collective language, we can learn to turn statements into questions – in other words, invitations.

There is a very different feeling between commands and invitations. Have you ever heard anyone get excited about being commanded? On the other hand, I've watched my kids get excited beyond control when they receive an invitation.

When you're the leader, the one in charge, it's far more natural – and far easier – to lecture and command than to discuss and invite. Leaders can create caste systems within their organizations simply by language choices. When they refer to "we" as the leadership team and "you" as the employees, they create a separation in the team. If we want our people to feel like they are in a partnership with us, that we are in it together, that we are locking arms with them to accomplish the overall goal of organizational success, then we need to communicate in a way that creates partnership.

The ultimate partner phrase is: "If I, will you …"

Example: "If I set aside time to help fine tune your board presentations, will you have it prepared by Friday to review?"

Example: "If I let you choose your people, will you head up the project?"

Example: "If I call XYZ Company and set up an appointment, will you prepare the background research to present to them?"

By saying "If I, will you ..." you are extending an invitation. It is a commitment on your part that naturally creates a commitment from the person you are addressing. It is not condescending, commanding or sharp. It is open, inviting and generates a feeling that we are in it together.

Learn to adopt this partnership phrase and not only will your communication feel more conversational, your people will feel included and respond with commitment.

Curious Not Critical

We've talked about the importance of speaking candidly to help others progress and improve. In this process we will inevitably deal with mistakes, problems, failures, setbacks, and stupid decisions.

I would suggest that as we deal with these mistakes and problems, a leader should be more curious than critical.

Natural human tendency leads to being pointedly critical. When something goes wrong, it's reflexive to respond with, "Are you kidding me?" "I can't believe you would do something so stupid." "You are an idiot!" "What were you thinking?!"

But does that help you or the person who made the mistake? No, in fact, it makes it worse because now they are offended and probably less likely to be cooperative or solution oriented.

Criticism that points out the obvious – that something went wrong – is not constructive. It doesn't build your people, make them feel safe, or allow them to learn. It causes them to be guarded, which creates a culture of secrets, avoidance, and cover-up.

If we take a deep breath and become curious, we can help the situation instead of exacerbating it.

Curiosity causes you to ask questions.
Criticism causes you to reprimand.
Curiosity seeks understanding.
Criticism seeks blame.
Curiosity builds trust and rapport.
Criticism builds resentment and defensiveness.
Curiosity focuses on the person.
Criticism focuses on the problem.
Curiosity creates partnerships.
Criticism creates divisions.
Curiosity leads to solutions.
Criticism leads to making others feel small and less confident.

Leaders who are curious are solution thinkers. They recognize mistakes and then seek to understand them, learn from them, and create a better future for everyone involved.

The company 3M has developed a culture of curiosity that has paid off. As a company that develops products, mistakes and failure are inevitable. How 3M deals with it is key to their success. Take the example of Spencer Silver, a 3M scientist who was working in his lab to develop a very strong adhesive. He wasn't successful, in fact, what he developed was a very weak adhesive. Instead of keeping this failure to himself for fear of how leadership would react, Spencer followed 3M's culture of sharing failures with others. Anther scientist Art Fry was in church choir practice some time later getting frustrated that he couldn't get his bookmark to stay in place when he remembered Silver's weak adhesive. That was the beginning of what would become a household name – Post-It Notes.

Not only was being curious and not critical key to the invention of Post-It Notes, it has impacted 3M's overall success and ability to develop products. The company currently holds more than twenty thousand patents and continues to develop products that we use everyday at a rate that most companies would only dream of. It's curiosity that fuels their success.

A mistake is just that – making a wrong judgment about something. Haven't we all done that? A mistake is not done with intention. Success is not accomplished by making others feel less than or to blame. In most cases people already feel bad enough. Can we as leaders extend an understanding and explore solutions together with our people?

Being critical also takes all of our energy and focuses in areas where we have no control. The mistake has been made and nothing is going to change that. When we are curious, we focus our attention on areas where we have control – solutions.

In partnership everyone wins – when we get there. Collectively working toward a solution gives ownership to the outcome. Mistakes require several things – understanding, correction and solutions.

So the next time a mistake comes your way – either your own or someone else's – will you be curious or critical?

Solution thinking

Thomas Jefferson said, "Nothing gives one person so much advantage over another as to remain always cool and unruffled under all circumstances." Curiosity aids our ability to control our emotions and focus on understanding and positive outcomes.

Part of solution thinking is to focus on the good. Being positive in a negative situation is not naïve – it's leadership.

Promote What you Love Instead of Bashing What You Hate
A few years ago I was speaking at a high school leadership conference in Wyoming. There were about three hundred teenagers in the audience and I talked to them about how they can be leaders and play to win in their life. After my speech several kids came up to me to thank me or tell me what they got out of the session, but there was one girl who stood back and waited for everyone to leave and then she approached me.

She asked if we could talk and we sat down at a table in the empty ballroom. She told me her name and said, "I'm struggling with something. I would like to get your advice." I asked her what it was and she said, "I am a lesbian and I don't feel like our country's laws are fair for people like me. Every day at school we stand up and say the pledge of allegiance and I feel like I should boycott this act because I can't support a country that doesn't support me. My parents don't want me to do this, but what do you think I should do?"

I was shocked at her question. It wasn't at all what I expected. But I knew what I wanted to teach her. My response had nothing to do with her being gay or straight. It wasn't political or religious. It is, however, the answer to some of the biggest problems we create for ourselves. I answered, "I'm not going to tell you what to believe or how to feel, but I do believe our world would be a better place if we started promoting what we love rather than bashing what we hate."

My advice was to focus not on what America isn't, but what it is – a place that champions freedom like no other, a place where you have rights and people bend over backwards to preserve them. Would it be positive if you boycotted the Pledge of Allegiance, if you embarrassed your parents? Why not concentrate instead on what's good about this country? Why not capitalize on that?

We had a great conversation about what that meant and how that is truly a principle of influence and persuasion and she left with a positive approach.

Now it is time for the rest of us to start promoting what we love instead of bashing what we hate.

There is no better example of this than in American politics. Campaigning has become such a mud-slinging exercise that you almost don't know what candidates stand for because all you hear from them is how bad their opponent is, or what's wrong instead of what's right.

But we do the same thing in business, don't we? We put down the competition and try to differentiate ourselves by talking about how we are better because they do this wrong and that wrong.

Let me ask you if that line of persuasion works on you. Do you become loyal to someone because they tell you how bad everyone else is? Of course not – so why do we lower ourselves to that standard?

If you want to stand out, be heard, be relevant, attract people to you, create change, and be an influence for good, promote what you love instead of bashing what you hate. As a leader, you will find your positivity will spread contagiously throughout your organization, resulting in an upbeat attitude that boosts morale and increases productivity.

STEP THREE: MAKING A CONNECTION

The word *communication* comes from the root word common. To truly communicate we need to find what we have in common. When we stand on common ground we are then in position to understand, relate and connect.

As leaders, two important ways we can find commonality and make strong connections with our people are *1)*, by not taking ourselves too seriously, and *2)*, by learning to tell a good story.

Laughter is a sure way of not taking ourselves too seriously

A few years ago we went with my family to our family cabin in Idaho. For one of the adventures we took the kids white water rafting in Jackson Hole, Wyoming. It was fantastic! On the way back to the cabin we stopped at Frosty Top to get some ice cream. We all ordered our ice cream or root beer floats and then sat outside and waited for it to be delivered. A teenage girl brought out all of our ice cream on a tray and as she reached across to hand someone their ice cream the tray slipped and she dumped an entire root beer float on the head of my eight-year-old daughter, Andie.

Andie was literally drenched in root beer float but much to my surprise – she laughed!

We all laughed after that and although the waitress felt horrible – Andie's laughter eased the tension and turned what could have easily been a horrible experience into a funny memory from our family trip.

That experience got me thinking about the power of laughter. I started to study laughter and came to appreciate that laughing doesn't just make things enjoyable, laughter is one of the most important parts of life, health, perspective, and leadership.

Here are 7 Powerful Things That Laughter Does to Make Life Better:

1. **Laughter dissolves distressing emotions.** You can't feel anxious, angry, or sad when you're laughing.
2. **Laughter helps you relax and recharge.** It reduces stress and increases energy, enabling you to stay focused and accomplish more.

3. **Humor shifts perspective, allowing you to see situations in a more realistic, less threatening light.** A humorous perspective creates psychological distance, which can help you avoid feeling overwhelmed.
4. **Laughter positively impacts health.** The simple act of laughing boosts immunity, decreases pain, relaxes muscles, and improves mood.
5. **Humor makes friends.** Humor strengthens relationships, attracts others to us, enhances teamwork, and promotes group bonding.
6. **Humor can ease embarrassing situations.** We all get embarrassed at times but being able to laugh at ourselves eases embarrassment and allow us to move forward.
7. **Laughter protects the heart.** Laughter improves the function of blood vessels and increases blood flow, which can help protect you against a heart attack and other cardiovascular problems.

Learning to find humor in any situation is a skill set and as you can see from the benefits listed above it is a crucial skillset to develop.

Abraham Lincoln struggled with bouts of depression and used humor as therapy. His ability to laugh at himself was revealed during a political debate when his opponent called him "two-faced." Lincoln replied, "I leave it to my audience. If I had another face, do you think I'd wear this one?"

Good humor truly is medicine to the soul. Humor can ease tension, relieve uncomfortable or embarrassing situations, change attitudes, generate love and understanding, and add sparkle to life.

Keep laughing!

Story-telling

Stories are a great way to make a connection. People love stories. People relate to stories. Stories are engaging, not only intellectually but also emotionally. When we hear a good story we automatically make a connection with the storyteller. As leaders we need to learn to tell a good story. In my book, "The Power of Storytelling" I break down the science and the art of telling a great story. For this section, let me synthesize that down to a couple of key points:

One: Don't talk too much.

I was recently interviewed by a business magazine about storytelling and leadership. One of the great questions they asked is what is the number one mistake leaders make when telling a story. The answer to this is simple: we talk too much.

There's a rule in storytelling that says if it's not necessary to say it becomes necessary not to say. As leaders, we often tell two-minute stories in five or ten minutes. That completely loses the connection we want to make with our audience. Jerry Seinfeld has said he will spend hours trying to take a six-word joke and make it five words long. The reason he does that is because he knows in comedy the quicker you get from the setup to the punch line the bigger the laugh. In storytelling the quicker we get to the point the more compelling the message is to the listener.

Two: Remember this formula – Struggle-to-Solution.

The setting, details, facts, and circumstances will vary, but the recipe for an influential story is simple. You hook people with the struggle, you help them with the solution.

There is something about trials, conflict, and adversity – the struggle – that engages us emotionally. It's human. We connect to it. We relate to it. We identify with it. And yet, I often see leaders tell stories that are solution-to-solution. They want to come across as powerful and without mistakes or blemishes, so they tell stories that say, in essence, we're great, we've always been great, and if you work with us it will be great.

But there's nothing engaging about that process. Struggle-to-solution stories are where leaders choose to be vulnerable and authentic. When you share examples of where you've been, what you've learned, and how you've changed and grown, those are the stories that truly make a connection.

A thoughtful, personal story that puts the listener's welfare first is one of the most effective ways for a leader to have a conversation that will prove both meaningful and powerfully connecting.

TY'S *TAKEAWAY*

- **The old adage said:**
  "When the leader talks – people listen."

- **In today's world:**
  "Leaders talk with people – not at people."

CHAPTER 6

PARTNER LEADERS UNDERSTAND THAT MOTIVATION IS IMPORTANT, BUT IT'S OVERRATED

Whenever you have a goal– whether that goal is to lose weight, make more money or, in this case, to have committed people – there are always two forces to consider: motivating forces that drive us to achieve our goal, and opposing forces, obstacles and inhibitors, that keep us away from our goal.

My question: which of these forces is more important?

While you consider that question, let me tell you a couple of stories:

Not too long ago I was sitting at my kitchen counter reading a text on my phone and our refrigerator was to the side of me. My son Drew said, "Dad, can you open the refrigerator for me?"

Drew is five years old and he knows how to open the refrigerator. So without looking up from my phone I said, "Drew, you can open the door." He then started crying and said,

"Dad, please, open the refrigerator." So I looked over and Drew was holding five or six Matchbox cars in his hands. At this point I had a choice. As his leader I could motivate him by saying, "Drew you can do it, try harder," or I could remove the obstacle and help him do his job. I said, "Drew, put the Matchbox cars down." He put them down. Then I said, "Open the fridge." He opened the fridge and yelled "Dad, I did it! I did it!"

Partner leaders understand that their role goes well beyond motivational cheerleading; their role is to foster a help – and solution-oriented relationship that benefits everyone involved. That principle applies not only in business, but in all walks of life.

I have a friend who struggled with depression, a cruel and often debilitating mental illness. He tried all sorts of ways to maintain a positive attitude, to keep busy, to be socially engaging, to be grateful – all the things that depression screams at you not to do but you know you need to do. Nothing seemed to help very much. It was only when we were able to help him understand depression – that it is a chemical imbalance that can be treated with medication that things began to change. With the right medication, depression became an identifiable obstacle and his therapies became more effective. All the moral support and encouragement in the world was not nearly as valuable as identifying the problem and addressing the best way to deal with it.

As a speaker I get calls virtually every day from people who say, "Ty we need you to come and motivate our people." In conversations with executives I'm often asked, "How do I motivate my people?" "How do we get them more excited, more committed?" My answer is always the same: motivation is important, but it's overrated.

As leaders, we're prone to spend all of our time focused on motivation when real leadership requires understanding our people, assessing the situation, and removing the obstacles and the inhibitors that keep them from doing their job well.

Motivation is important, it needs to be there, but it's overrated because we focus too much time on the pep talk and not enough time on the performance beyond the pep talk.

Force Field Analysis

An MIT psychologist named Kurt Lewin is often called the father of social psychology. It was his research that resulted in Force Field Analysis, a formula that explains why people – and businesses – either stay in the same place or move in a new direction. He postulated that, "An issue is held in balance by the interaction of two opposing sets of forces – those seeking to promote change and those attempting to maintain the status quo."

In other words, if the driving forces and the restraining forces are equal, it's like pushing the brake and the gas pedal at the same time. The vehicle isn't going anywhere.

Only when the power to move outweighs the power to remain stationary does progress happen.

The simplicity of the analytic lends itself to an easy-to-understand diagram. In the drawing below, the goal is in the middle, flanked on one side by all the factors that will propel you toward it and on the other side by all the inhibitors that will keep you from it.

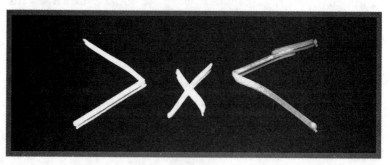

Leaders understand that clearly identifying goals and identifying all the reasons they can and cannot be achieved is essential to getting everyone on board and looking in the same direction. The problem that most leaders have is that they spend most of their time on one side of the diagram. They look at ways to motivate their people or wonder why they're not motivated enough to get the job done.

Spending time dealing with the opposing forces means identifying and removing obstacles and inhibitors, providing training, and individualizing our approach. It often takes a little more work. But it's more than worth it. The leaders who remove obstacles and inhibitors for their people and increase the capacity for them to do their job well end up with very motivated people who are committed to achieving the goal.

Clearly identifying the obstacle is key. Imagine Sir Edmund Hillary and Tenzing Norgay on May 31, 1953 when they were within 300 feet of the top of Mount Everest, at 29,035 feet the highest point on earth. In front of them stood a 40-foot wall of rock and ice that Hillary later described as "a formidable looking problem … that might well spell the difference between success and failure."

Hillary spent some time studying the sheer wall until he identified a small crack between a ridge of ice and rock. He wedged his feet, hands and shoulders into the crack and shinnied upward. Forty feet later, he looked down at his companion, tossed him a rope, and together they climbed the remaining 300 feet to become the first men to stand on top of the world. Ever since, climbers who summit Everest on the popular southeast route surmount with confidence the sheer rock face known as the Hillary Step – named for the leader who showed the way beyond it.

Training

Partner leaders focus on coaching, on training, on mentoring, and on equipping. On making your people better.

Why?

Because when people are really good at what they do they will show up and do it every single day.

They need to know what to do and they need to know how to do it. That's where real self-esteem comes from. When somebody can be amazing at what they do, they will do it at a higher level.

A study by IBM showed that in organizations that rate high in performance, 84 percent of employees are receiving the training they need, compared with just 16 percent in companies that rate low in performance.

"Top performing companies not only recognize the importance of their people, but also the need to provide the right skills to enable their people," said the report, which went on to say, "Seventy-one percent of CEOs cited human capital, ahead of products, customer relationships and brands, as the leading source of sustained economic value."

That thinking was corroborated by an International Journal of Science and Research article that called training "crucial for organization development and success." Effective workplace training, the report found, results in many benefits, including:

- **Improved morale.**
- **Less supervision.**
- **Fewer accidents.**
- **Promotions from within.**
- **Increased productivity.**

As companies, we need to recognize the importance of investing in training for the overall commitment, performance, and effectiveness of your people and as leaders we need to take that responsibility on our own shoulders to partner with our people in a way that helps to make them better every day. I come across many companies and many leaders who see training as an unnecessary expense or as a distraction from the real work that needs to be done. That view is unfortunate because it undermines the outcome that they're looking for. True wealth is ability. Give your people the ability to do their job unbelievably well and they will show up and do it unbelievably well every single day.

A numbers game

In my previous life – haha, in my twenties – my brother and I built a large business in direct sales. We had a substantial sales team that focused on selling nutritional supplements through doctors' offices. In the direct-sales industry there are a couple of sayings that have become almost universally accepted.

One is "Some will. Some won't. So what? Next."

The other is "You can't say the right thing to the wrong person and you can't say the wrong thing to the right person."

In essence, they're saying that it's a numbers game. It's volume that matters. Quantity over quality. Your presentation isn't that important, it's how many times you give it that's important. The more people you talk to, the better your chance of success.

For several years I bought into that philosophy, but at some point I began to realize that it preaches the wrong doctrine, that such thinking takes away the responsibility to be better. If you constantly dismiss your failure as an indication of the industry as a whole, you alleviate yourself of the challenges to engage the prospect, present with persuasion, and move people forward.

We realized that persistence doesn't matter unless performance improves. So we began to train our people differently. Instead of simply giving sales ideas and providing motivation, we began to do in-depth training that involved interactive role-playing and the development of people skills. We analyzed what approaches got the best results and what approaches were less effective and passed that along to the sales force.

All of our sales people began to record every presentation they gave and to go back and analyze those with the intent of learning how they sounded and where they could improve. We developed training manuals and a training website that went in depth on every aspect of product knowledge as well as presentation skills. Our sales team became amazing at asking questions, at assessing a prospect's needs, and individualizing the presentation to fit those needs.

As we made our people better, the numbers game changed. It's not that we weren't willing to do the volume, we still worked hard and did the numbers, but after the change in training, our percentages got better.

The formula works. Training + Time = Goals.

A client of mine, Centegra Health Care Systems of Illinois, recently asked me to work with their leadership over a several month period. When I met with the executive team, I asked them to describe the role of their managers, which is the group I was going to be working with.

Their response was, "Our managers' job is to remove obstacles so that things flow smoothly."

And it showed. As I got to know the company that includes over 4,000 employees I could see that the strength of the organization was in the careful attention the managers paid to making sure their people were well trained and had excellent working conditions. It was no surprise that Centegra successfully gained approval from the state to open just the second new hospital in Illinois in the past 30 years.

A partner leader motivates, he inspires, he leads by example, but more importantly, he helps his people do their job well. He makes them better.

TY'S *TAKEAWAY*

- **The old adage said,
  "Great leaders are great motivators."**

- **In today's world, "Great leaders know
  that helping people do their job well
  is the ultimate motivation."**

CULTURE
EATS STRATEGY
FOR LUNCH

CHAPTER 7

PARTNER LEADERS
RECOGNIZE THAT
CULTURE EATS
STRATEGY FOR LUNCH

Howard Schultz, the famed chairman of Starbucks, recently told his leadership team that, "Culture eats strategy for lunch."

Do you think that is true?

I don't believe Schultz was saying that strategy is unimportant. Howard bought Starbucks when they were one small coffee shop in Seattle and has overseen the growth of more than 15,000 stores in 53 countries, becoming a recognizable name worldwide. He has a strategy and it works.

I think what he was saying is that business has changed. Having a great strategy, product or service is no longer a competitive advantage. Everyone is good. That's the entry fee. So what separates the greats? It's culture. It's the way their people show up. The commitment they give. The ownership they take. The engagement they exercise.

Your culture will be your catalyst to outperform the competition and provide the type of service that creates loyalty. It's what takes you from success to significance in the eyes of your customers.

The old adage said that leadership is what drove business, but in today's world, culture drives business. As the leader, your job is to embody, encourage and inspire the culture of your organization.

Carly Fiorina said, "Leadership is about challenging the status quo, solving problems, producing results, and the highest calling of all leadership is to unlock the potential in others." That is what a culture of commitment does; it empowers others. The right culture makes people feel valued, establishes the values that will enable success, provides purpose and pushes people to do their very best.

Culture

Culture has become the hot word in business today. A lot has been written on the subject, with many examples of who has gotten it right.

As I have studied the culture of hundreds of organizations, I have found that successful cultures are often very different from each other. They value and believe different things and yet each is finding success. So instead of giving you the formula for building the perfect culture (because I am not sure there is a universal formula) I want to instead warn you of five mistakes that leaders often make that kill culture.

They are:

1. **Hire For the Wrong Reasons**
2. **Focus on Tasks and Not Purpose**
3. **Preach Values That You Don't Live**
4. **Incentivize the Wrong Activities**
5. **Not Investing in Your Culture**

1. Hire For the Wrong Reasons

Terrell Owens was a great football talent. He played fifteen seasons in the National Football League, was named All-Pro five times, caught more passes than all but five players in NFL history, and is the only player ever to score two or more touchdowns against all 32 franchises. That's the bright side of the story. The problem was fitting into a team. Owens played for the San Francisco 49ers, Philadelphia Eagles, Dallas Cowboys, Buffalo Bills and Cincinnati Bengals – five different franchises – and was released by every one of them because of some kind of controversy or conflict. Every time the pattern repeated itself. Lured by his immense skill set, teams continued to bet they could handle his me-first attitude, only to find out it wasn't worth it.

As I've talked with numerous successful CEOs about culture, every single one of them has said something to the effect that you hire for attitude and you train for position. A sure way to kill culture is by trying to force something to fit that has the potential to ruin morale. (Owens once led the Cincinnati Bengals in receptions, yards and touchdowns for the season, but after a 4-12 won-lost record they still let him go). In the hiring process, prospects obviously need to have the skill set necessary for the position, but we also need to look at who they are, the values that they profess, and do they fit into our culture. Will they add to it or take away from it? Ability alone isn't enough to sustain culture.

2. Focus on Tasks and Not Purpose

The object of this book is to teach the leadership approach that creates commitment from your people. Nothing more, nothing less. Committed people get more done, do it better, and make a bigger impact.

In Chapter 1, I said that people aren't committed to jobs or companies, they are committed to people. Leaders who are seen as honest, authentic, genuine, caring, and fully invested will attract a loyal, dedicated following. But wise leaders know there's more to the commitment equation. Equally as powerful is purpose. When people don't feel like they are performing a task, but instead feel like they are changing the world – they will feel inspired. When they see the why as well as the how, their commitment grows. Partner leaders focus on establishing a purpose and engaging the team around that. Tasks drive the bare minimum, but a sense of purposefulness drives going well above and beyond.

My friend, Cindy, told me a story that every leader who wants to create a strong culture needs to heed and understand.

Several years ago Cindy and her kids noticed that two robins had built a nest in one of their trees. As they paid attention to the robins' activity they realized there were eggs in the nest. Those eggs soon hatched four baby birds.

Cindy and her kids took ownership of the baby birds. They loved to watch them and would check on their condition regularly.

Then one day as Cindy was putting clothes away in one of the kid's rooms – she saw something she'd never seen before or since. More then a dozen birds were flying around the tree with the robin's nest. Cindy rushed out to see what all the fuss was about and saw all different types of birds were attacking the tree. Instinctively, Cindy ran to protect the baby birds and what she found was amazing.

The birds were dive-bombing the tree because a snake had wrapped itself around the tree and was trying to get to the baby robins. The birds were doing everything they could do attack the snake and save the baby birds.

Cindy thought quickly and grabbed a shovel and used it to pull the snake off the tree. It slithered away and when Cindy eventually turned around all of the birds were sitting on the branches of the tree looking at her as if to say thank you. Then they flew away.

So what does this story have to do with culture?

There is something amazing that happens when we have a common cause. When we have a common enemy, just like the birds, we forget our differences. We begin to collaborate and focus on common objectives and we fight for our cause.

As leaders trying to establish a strong culture, it is important to establish your values and beliefs. By defining what you believe and who your common enemy is – you bring people together to fight for a cause.

Companies that have been praised for their cultures understand their cause and it brings them together. They live their values, share common beliefs and fight against their common enemy. Zappos is fighting mediocrity in customer service. Target is fighting to democratize designer fashions. Southwest Airlines is fighting to make the travel experience fun. Each of these examples feature leaders who have helped to create a culture where a common enemy brings their people together to fight a cause.

Leaders do not drive business – culture does. Leadership's job is to create and maintain a positive culture that has a mission that is clearly defined and understood by all.

P.S. – To not leave you hanging, the baby birds were saved.

3. Preach Values That You Don't Live

As important as it is for leaders to preach the values and beliefs of the group, it is paramount that they live those values and beliefs themselves. One of the fastest ways to kill a culture is for members of the organization to see a leader break the rules or not follow the values that they profess. It erodes trust, kills partnership and creates a free-for-all mentality that destroys morale and teamwork. On the flip side, when leaders live the values and beliefs they profess, people adopt those values as well.

After a recent speech on partner leadership I received this email:

> Truly enjoyed your talk yesterday at C&A in Omaha. I am fortunate to work for a company whose leadership has always practiced partnership and I have a perfect example to share. Feel free to talk about it as you wish!
>
> As a Midwest commercial general contractor and contract furniture dealer, we were hit hard by the recession of 2008/2009. Clients pushed work back, some clients stopped all work, new business was non-existent ... you remember the drill. We hunkered down, focused on our existing clients and didn't lay anyone off.
>
> By April 2010, with little work in sight, and not wanting to go into debt, our leadership team (12 of us) decided to implement an across the board 10% salary cut for all salaried employees (about 50 people out of 100 employees). Hourly wages were not cut. As the year progressed, work picked up and things looked brighter. Employees felt that we would gain back that 10% before long.
>
> Here's what happened on December 10th of that year – eight months later: Our owners called an emergency

meeting of all salaried personnel, they thanked us for the generous "loan," reinstituted our original salaries, and (are you ready?) PAID US BACK WITH INTEREST! Two weeks before Christmas. Amazing.

Now that's leadership as partnership. Did I say I was fortunate to work here? 25 years with the same Company (at least ten different roles), and we have many folks who have been here 10, 15, 20 years.

When I was interviewing Brian Wheeler, the founder of Tijuana Flats Burrito Company, for this book, I love what he had to say about leaders embodying the values they profess. He said, "There isn't fake culture – you have to feel it inside your soul. You have to believe. Do you hurt when they hurt and are you happy when they are happy? If so, your team will follow you anywhere."

As leaders, we need to be the culture that we profess. We need to live it in every way and then we have the authority to preach it to our people.

I've found that one of the best ways for leaders to reinforce what they stand for and what they truly believe is through storytelling. We discussed storytelling in Chapter Five, but it can also be a powerful way to spread company culture. The stories you tell reinforce the values that are important. For example, if your organization has a culture that stresses growth from within, telling stories about a supervisor who started out as a janitor, or a CFO whose first position was as an intern in the accounting department, is an excellent way to reinforce that company value. Such stories become part of the company lore and authenticate the culture you are trying to keep and protect.

I encourage leaders to pay attention to the culture stories they are telling, making sure that they fall in line with core values. But above all: Storydoing is more important than storytelling. Leadership is spelled **E X A M P L E.**

4. Incentivize the Wrong Activities

It's not only what leaders preach and what they live, but we also need to think about what we incentivize. What type of behaviors and what type of focus do our promotions, our bonuses, and our incentive trips create? Are they productive or are they counter-productive? For example, if your company preaches that customer service is the most important thing that you do, then incentivizing your customer services reps for the number of calls that they take in a day kills your culture.

At a financial adviser group that is a client of mine, their sales force is comprised of all independent reps. Since there are no restrictions on territory and all prospective clients are fair game to all, competition can become pretty cutthroat. To counteract that and foster the one-for-all-and-all-for-one culture the organization espouses, leadership instituted a program where a percentage of salaries come from the collective whole. If everyone is doing well, there's a reward tied to it that comes from collaborating and doing well together.

A wise partner leader knows that incentives need to motivate the whole rather than a select few.

5. Not investing in your culture

In an interview with Jim Crystal, the CEO of Revelry Agency, a public relations and online digital presence company, he said he sees too many leaders now that think get-togethers, retreats, and any other activities outside of the workplace are a waste of time. But Jim firmly believes that the extra events are what cement your culture. Taking time to create an atmosphere that develops relationships, builds trust, and strengthens the team is invaluable to fashioning the environment you desire.

Jim loves Sun Valley, Idaho. It's a beautiful destination resort town, with fun activities both in the winter and the summer. Jim always makes it a point to take his entire team to Sun Valley to spend a few days together. There are business meetings and seminars, but there's also plenty of time left to relax and enjoy one another while doing everything from skiing to fishing to bike riding to hiking to horseback riding to golfing. What does this accomplish? If you look at the people who work at Revelry Agency, most of them have been there a very long time. The continuity is pretty remarkable, and I think a lot of it has to with the Sun Valley getaways and all the other investments Jim has made in creating a culture people don't want to leave. It's no wonder *Outside Magazine* ranked Revelry in the top 30 places to work in the U.S. two years in a row.

In a bottom-line world, it's easy for leaders to neglect investing in their culture. Expenditures for team-building events, especially those outside the office, can be easily dismissed as not absolutely needed, so therefore put off, sometimes forever. Plus, everyone's busy and it takes time, energy and effort to put together retreats, activities, banquets, picnics and other events that are thoughtful, meaningful, and designed to produce the desired results. They don't just happen.

But forgetting to prioritize people over processes is never a good idea. If we truly want a culture of committed and engaged individuals, then we need to be willing to do everything possible to create an environment that puts people first. The positive results will follow.

TY'S *TAKEAWAY*

- **The old adage said: "Leadership drives business."**

- **In today's world: "Culture drives business and the leader's job is to inspire and embody that culture."**

CHAPTER 8

PARTNER LEADERS CREATE LEADERS NOT FOLLOWERS

What Defines Leadership?

Who is the best football coach in the history of the National Football League? If we were to go by who has won the most Super Bowls, it is tie between Chuck Noll and Bill Belichick, who have both won four Super Bowls. If we were to judge by winning percentage, Vince Lombardi is the best coach ever with a won-lost percentage of .740.

But if we judge football coaches as leaders, is winning percentage or titles the correct barometer? Is it fair to judge a leader simply by the number of followers they have – like a popularity contest? Or is the ideal standard based on bottom line revenue and growth?

The question isn't who won the most games in the NFL or who won the most Super Bowls in the NFL – the question is who is the best coach in the history of the NFL? In other words – who is the best leader? And to determine true leadership, I don't think it is about winning or followers, it is about leaders building leaders. Ralph Nader said, "The function of leadership is to produce other leaders, not other followers."

Partner leadership is about legacy. It is about empowerment. It is about creating commitment in our people, giving them an ownership mentality and inspiring them to step up and contribute at the highest level.

If we are to judge based on this standard then we need to look at the best coach question in an entirely different light.

A coaching tree is similar to a family tree except that it shows the relationships of coaches instead of family members. There are several different ways to define a relationship between two coaches. The most common way to make the distinction is if a coach worked as an assistant on a particular head coach's staff for at least a season then that coach can be counted as being a branch on the head coach's coaching tree.

Coaching trees are common in the National Football League and most coaches in the NFL can trace their lineage back to a certain head coach for whom they previously worked as an assistant.

A coaching tree doesn't just show winning percentages or Super Bowls, it also shows the leaders the coach has created and what they have done in turn.

So, who is the best football coach in the history of the National Football League? In terms of a coaching tree, there is one obvious winner – Bill Parcells.

Parcells is part of the NFL Hall of Fame. He won two Super Bowls and coached in one additional Super Bowl. But Coach Parcells is more than his own statistics because he doesn't just leave behind a coaching tree, he helped grow a Super Bowl-era Sequoia.

Parcells and his disciples, Bill Belichick, Tom Coughlin and Sean Payton, have combined to win eight of 47 Super Bowls – the sturdiest, most prolific coaching tree in league history. Parcells reflects like a father on those shimmering Lombardi trophies – three by Belichick, two by Coughlin and one by Payton – hoisted by those with whom he shared his most prized team-building and coaching secrets.

Bill Parcells is the Coach of Coaches or, in other words, the Leader of Leaders in the National Football League. He was extremely successful but his leadership has carried on long after him because of the leaders he has produced.

Jack Welch ... What is Your Legacy?

As celebrity CEO's go, Jack Welch is at or near the top of the list. During his time running General Electric in the 1980s and 1990s the company grew from $26.8 billion in revenue to $130 billion, making it the largest company in the world before his departure. By that standard Jack Welch was a great leader. But what happens when the standard isn't simply bottom line results?

If you were to look at the trajectory of the S&P 500 during the same time frame that GE's revenues were skyrocketing, it actually matches the growth of GE, making the company's rise, while still significant, less remarkable. The U.S. economy was thriving and most companies experienced tremendous growth as a result. That's not to say that Jack Welch wasn't brilliant at developing systems to maximize revenue or foster short term growth, I just believe we need to look at leadership with a different measuring stick.

In "Leaders Eat Last," Simon Sinek observed, "Great companies and great leaders are ones able to succeed beyond any one leader and manage through the hard times. What if we judge a leader not on what they do when they are holding the torch but on what happens after they pass it on? On that metric, Welch doesn't fare so well. A leader's legacy is only as strong as the foundation they leave behind that allows others to continue to advance the organization in their name. Legacy is not the memory of better times when the older leader was there. That's not legacy, that is nostalgia."

Jack Welch built GE not to last but to maximize the opportunity of the day. And the fall of GE was long and hard after his departure.

My Experiment

The question becomes: How do you produce other leaders? And if our focus is on empowerment and leadership development, then the legacy of a leader is not what they do when they are at the helm, but rather what happens after they leave.

Two years ago, with this thought process in place, I had a chance to test out some of my theories on leadership and can now measure the results.

In June of 2013, I was put in as president of the Mountain West Chapter of The National Speakers Association. This position was a one year commitment and I wanted to not only make an impact during that year but I wanted to set up a structure for the chapter that would help it continue to thrive after my term was completed.

I had a board of 10 people who were amazing, but they were all frustrated and not extremely committed. That wasn't a reflection on them as much as it was a reflection on the situation.

The president the year before I took over was very committed, but she didn't listen to others' opinions or allow others to take ownership and it had taken its toll. This was how the board felt and since I was not involved at this level before, it was my job to listen and collectively find a solution for success, to move forward together and create something as a group that worked. The chapter was financially solvent but with little savings in the bank. We were operating basically paycheck to paycheck. This was another concern for long-term sustainability.

With that picture in mind, let me tell you what I did.

I believe that leadership is built on genuine relationships. So my first order of business was to reach out personally to every member of the board. I heard their frustrations, listened to their ideas and gained their trust. Most of these conversations were more than an hour long, but I had to help them to see that this year was going to be different, that their voices would be heard and that they would be part of a team. The time invested in each individual worked, and I gained their commitment. Individual investment in your people is a must if you want to develop leaders.

Next, I solicited their ideas and polled the membership as a whole to see what ideas/changes people were looking for. I firmly believe that *people support what they help create* and so we identified three major initiatives that a large group of people wanted. One of the initiatives was designed to fill a need but would also be a revenue source and could solve our financial situation.

As a board, we developed a very clear plan that we communicated to the chapter as a whole and it was met with excitement. Not only had the ideas come from the people, but we had a clear plan that benefited everyone involved and solved the main needs that people shared with us.

With these three new initiatives, we created systems. I have always believed that if you are going to do something more than once, you need a system. A system allows it to be duplicated.

I knew that strong leadership was going to be key to long-term success, so I wanted to make sure I took the time to mentor the incoming president. We went to breakfast monthly, I took him to a basketball game and I brought him on a retreat that I was putting on so that I could spend one-on-one time with him to make sure he was ready to take on the responsibility of the chapter the next year. Followers become leaders through mentorship.

I think one of the reasons that leaders don't duplicate leadership is because they love the limelight too much. We all have an ego to some extent; I know I do. But I truly wanted the chapter to thrive after my year was over, so I made sure to allow others to run the meetings, act as emcee and be the face of the chapter as much as possible. With every meeting I asked one of the board members to run the meeting and serve as emcee. I spent time with that person in preparation and then I turned it over to them. We had 11 meetings that year and I ran one of them. Each member of the board ran one as well. People need opportunities to practice – growth comes from new opportunities and responsibility.

I am happy to report that during my year as chapter president we nearly doubled the membership. We increased the attendance at our meetings by 40 percent. We implemented the first speaker school in our chapter's history and due to its success and the increased attendance, we ended the year with more than a year's operating cost in savings. The other two initiatives were very successful and our vision for the year was achieved and then some.

In writing this I am not trying to get credit for the success of the chapter, nor do I claim credit for what took place during my year as president. We had a very engaged board that did amazing things to accomplish what we did.

I approached this leadership opportunity as a case study to see what principles create leaders and not followers and I wanted to share some of the principles with you.

My evidence is not what happened during my year as president. My evidence is what has happened since I stepped down.

Over the year that followed my presidency, I have had very little involvement. My travel schedule has been such that I have only been to two meetings. So I truly have stepped away.

The chapter however, is doing better than ever. The board is engaged, the president is doing a great job, and the membership has increased another 40 percent over our doubling the year before. The second year of the speaker school was an even bigger success and that has allowed the chapter to now have nearly three years of savings in the bank. The attendance at meetings has increased by an additional 25 percent and the future looks bright.

What Does It Take?

Based on my experience and studying other leaders who have left a legacy of leadership, I have realized that there are some key steps to empowering your people and building leaders not followers.

They are:
- **Build relationships with key people**
- **Raise the vision of your people**
- **Create systems for anything you will do more than once**
- **Give them the opportunity to step up**
- **Mentor individually**
- **Reinforce We not Me**

Build relationships with key people

In chapter two we talked about the value of developing relationships with those you lead. I can't stress the importance of that enough. Leaders are in the people business first and foremost. Understanding that one concept will ensure success both long term and short term more than any other. No one should be ignored or left out in establishing relationships, but it's also important to identify those with potential to lead the organization in the future and develop a leadership-in-training relationship with them.

These are the people who will one day assume command, the key people who will ensure continuity. They need to be singled out and nurtured. As a leader, you need to regularly schedule opportunities to foster this relationship. That may be over breakfast, lunch or dinner, or in some other consistent setting that makes sense. They need to be shown their potential. The philosopher Goethe said, "Treat people as if they were what they ought to be, and you help them to become what they are capable of becoming." The relationships you develop with future leaders of the organization should be tailored with the view that these are the people who will succeed you.

Raise the vision of your people

In Chapter Four we talked about how important it is for leaders to not only be clear about their vision and be able to communicate it properly, but just as important is to involve people in the process.

Including your people in planning and decision-making opens their eyes and makes them feel an important part in achieving goals and objectives. Have you ever sat in the pilot's seat in a big passenger airplane? The view is very different than the one from a seat in the coach section. It is expansive and panoramic and all encompassing. Unless there are clouds, you can see exactly where you're going. Perceptive partner leaders let their people into the cockpit from time to time and give them a clear picture of what the leader is seeing and where they are going.

Nothing creates an ownership or leadership mindset like seeing things from the leader's perspective.

Create systems for anything you will do more than once

If we want success to be duplicated and repeated we need to spend a little more time as we develop new programs and put together new initiatives to create a system that allows others to duplicate what we've done. The old mentality of leadership was to just hope that the next guy would be as good as we were, but long term sustainability requires a more deliberate approach.

A system does not need to be complicated, but if the steps are clearly outlined and communicated the process can be repeated over and over without a change in quality or results. Great partner leaders do not operate in a vacuum, they document how and why they do what they do and clearly communicate that to those who will one day take their place.

Give them the opportunity to step up

According to research conducted by Dr. Natalia Lorinkova, who studies management and leadership at Wayne State University, "Teams led by a directive leader initially outperform those led by an empowering leader. However, despite lower early performance, teams led by an empowering leader experience higher performance improvement over time because of higher levels of team-learning, coordination, empowerment and mental model development."

If we want to be successful long term in business, then we need to empower others. And we need to do so on a regular basis. It might be easier to do it yourself – because of your experience and years of practice, it often is – but allowing others to take the lead invests them and gives them ownership. Wise partner leaders get to know their people well so they can appreciate what opportunities are within their reach and allow them to develop leadership qualities that will serve them and the organization well in the future.

Mentor individually

We talked above about identifying leaders for the future. Mentoring is how to get them there. A mentor is "an experienced and trusted adviser," one who shows the way. It isn't bragging or showing off. John Wooden said, "Mentoring isn't about celebrating your own insight but about sharing wisdom. When you pass on the lessons of your life with someone else, it's not you who are teaching – it's your experience."

To mentor individually means to pay attention to each person's interests, desires and capabilities, to recognize that everyone doesn't fit the same mold, and wisdom is most effectively shared one-on-one.

Mentoring is an investment in your people. It requires time, energy and effort on the part of the leader.

My friend Don Yaeger, who coauthored *The Two Most Important Days of Your Life* with me, used to write for *Sports Illustrated*. While he was at SI he heard that John Wooden was mentoring Shaquille O'Neal (who played for the Lakers at the time) and he thought there might be an interesting story in their relationship. So Don called Shaq and asked if he could sit in on their mentoring session. Shaq agreed and Don spent the day with O'Neal, one of the best basketball players in the world, and Wooden, one of the greatest coaches the game has ever known. What amazed him is they talked about everything. Life, kids, marriage, and basketball. At the end of the day, Don asked Coach Wooden, "Coach, why did you agree to mentor Shaq?" Coach Wooden simply said, "Because he asked."

After Don returned to Florida and wrote the story, he called Coach Wooden and said, "Coach, I feel like I need to ask." Coach Wooden slyly replied, "It's about time."

That began a twelve-year mentoring relationship where Don would fly to California once a month and spend a day with his mentor. He recorded thousands of hours of conversation and advice from arguably the best basketball mind on the planet. Don would tell you, though; he was an even better man.

Coach John Wooden was a leader of leaders whose legacy lives on in those he mentored. Don Yaeger and hundreds of others who learned at the feet of John Wooden benefited greatly from his wisdom and experience, and even more greatly from his willingness to give of his time and his energy to others.

Reinforce "We" not "Me"

There is no I in team – or in leader. The art of partner leadership is to communicate in terms of "we" not "me," of "us" not "them." The goal is to always be inclusive, not exclusive.

Partner leaders take blame when things go wrong and give credit to the team when things go right. They praise others openly, have the tough conversations privately, and reinforce the team concept. They see themselves as a leader of leaders and not as the spokesperson, the one in charge, or the celebrity. They realize that leadership is not about you as the leader – it is about the people you lead. They do their best to keep their ego at bay and to give themselves fully to their people and their organization.

They do all of these things not because it makes them look better but because they realize that when you reinforce we not me, you grow leaders. That is how you build a legacy and leave your organization better for having had you as a leader.

TY'S *TAKEAWAY*

- **The old adage said:
  "Become a leader that is irreplaceable."**

- **In today's world: "The real test of leadership
  is the ability to create leaders, not followers."**

A
RALLYING
CRY

CHAPTER 9

A RALLYING CRY

Partnership is the new leadership is the rallying cry for effective leadership in today's world. In the 1980s, Ken Blanchard changed the conversation from management to leadership and began to refocus, retool, and refine the approach to leadership. Our world has continued to change since then and at an even faster pace. To be relevant, influential, and successful today, partnership in leadership needs to be the approach.

The old adage said leadership was based on title, position, and authority, but that's not true in today's world. Title does not give you the right to be heard, value does. In today's world, people don't want to be talked at, they want to be talked with. Partner leaders approach leadership by building relationship, adding value, involving their people and communicating in a conversational manner. That's what makes them more than motivators, but instead the type of leaders that make people better, the type of leaders that create buy-in and the type of leaders that inspire a culture of commitment.

What every leader says they want from their people is commitment, but the truth is, the ultimate commitment is when our people step up as leaders themselves, when they take an ownership mentality, when they see the same vision we see and act accordingly. The ultimate goal of partner leadership is to create more leaders. That is not only what today's world needs, but also what it demands.